TAPESTRY WEAVING
for beginners and beyond

CREATE GRAPHIC WOVEN ART WITH
THIS GUIDE TO PAINTING WITH YARN

KRISTIN CARTER

DAVID & CHARLES

www.davidandcharles.com

Contents

Welcome to Weaving!

Woohoo! And welcome to the introduction. Many different crafters may hold this book in their hot little hands so here's what I've got for you: perhaps this is your first try at weaving, and to that I say welcome! This book will start you off with the basics, giving you an idea how to dip your toe into the world of weaving without having to invest hundreds in a fancy loom, bespoke tools etc. I think I used a fork from the kitchen drawer for my first year of weaving, so there is no shame in starting low tech and ramping up as your interest grows. There's also no shame in discount store acrylic yarn while you're getting a handle on things, and no shame in copying projects while you find your own style. This book is about not taking things too seriously. The overarching message: if that's what you like it, go for it.

If you've already had a go at this weaving caper and are looking to add some new skills to your repertoire, this book can help you there too. After learning the basic steps of weaving from tutorials and websites, I felt like the standard weaving pieces that you see around just weren't doing it for me, so I experimented with different ways to create pieces that I liked – bold graphic illustrations, detailed intricate images, chunky relaxed textures. There are always new places to take this artform, and I hope you will be able to learn a few here and transpose them into your work.

Finally, please don't expect this book to be your typical 'make this piece for yourself' craft book. There are a few projects that you can copy straight from the page, but I'm much more interested in holding your hand while you learn how to create your own pieces for your own space. Translate what is in this book to what suits your style. If you're anything like me, you've tried a thousand different mediums and have a craft drawer or cupboard that is a roadmap of creativity. Weaving is one artform with so much flexibility and where a bunch of different mediums converge into one. You'll get to illustrate and sketch up ideas for your designs, play with balancing colour and matching the feel to your home, you'll dive into the wonderful world of yarn and fibre and get the chance to embrace the textures and finishes that feel right to you. And at the end of the day, you're making things for you, so GO FOR IT! Good luck and happy making.

Tools

The old proverb 'a bad carpenter blames his tools' is one thing, but with weaving there's a little more forgiveness. The beauty is that much of your current tool stash can be pressed into use, many items will already be familiar, with a few exceptions. That strange comb thing is called a beater. Sure, purchase one if you want, but I used a kitchen fork to start with and I survived. You'll need a thick weaving needle (I prefer metal over plastic), and an extra-long tapestry needle is handy too. Large and small scissors have their place, but if it can snip through a piece of yarn, they'll be fine. Dowel is great for hanging your pieces, but driftwood or scavenged branches work too. I use balsa wood as my shed stick, but for that first year, a ruler was my friend. So you see – you can make weaving fit you. And I hope you do.

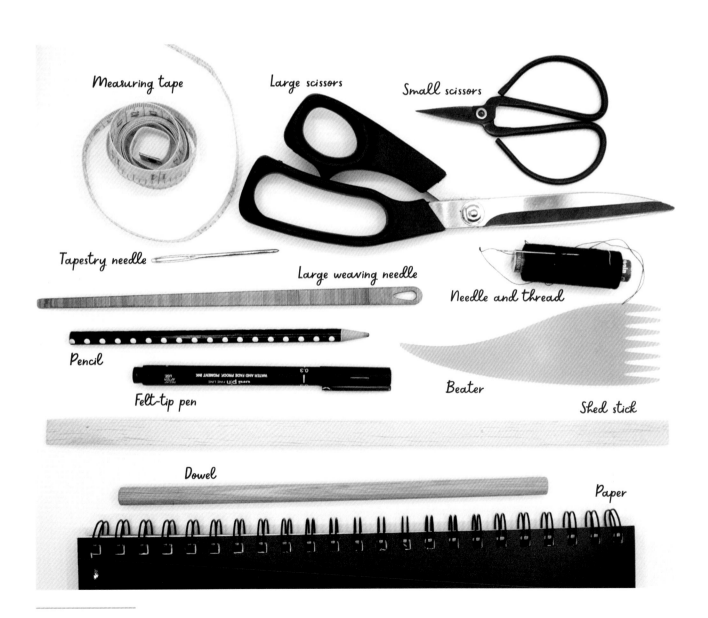

Measuring tape

Large scissors

Small scissors

Tapestry needle

Large weaving needle

Needle and thread

Pencil

Felt-tip pen

Beater

Shed stick

Dowel

Paper

Making Your Loom

The first step on this weaving journey is to make yourself a loom. If you're one of the lucky ducks that has their own, hurray for you, but these designs rely heavily on keeping a piece of paper adhered right behind your warp strings, so if your loom doesn't let you do that, perhaps you might want to get a little handy and make your own. To those loomless wanderers out there – you're obviously keen enough on weaving to buy a book about it, so I assume you'd like a loom that will last.

This design will transition with you from template guided weaving as shown in this book, to freehand weaving, and can be re-made into different sizes as you catch the weaver fever.

The choice of nail is the clincher in this, as you want something with a bullet or pin head, not a wide, flat head. When it comes time to take your work off the loom, you want something that isn't going to snag and pull the tension out of all your hard work. That said – let's begin.

TO CONSIDER

> The templates in this book are set to an A3 paper size, so find an A2-size picture frame or an A3-size poster frame

> Make sure the frame surround is timber, not plastic

> Make sure the frame width is wide enough so that the nails will have enough room to be staggered

> A chunky frame that sits deep off the glass will make it harder to follow your templates, so find something relatively shallow

YOU WILL NEED

- A2-size timber picture frame, 44 x 61cm (17¼ x 24in)
- Approx 200 bullet head nails with a smooth shank, 20–25mm (1–1½in) length, 1.25mm (4D) diameter, I used a pack of 460 nails for this project and had plenty left over
- Small hammer
- Masking/washi tape (optional)
- Tape measure
- Pencil

1. Remove the backing and glass from your picture frame, and turn it over to check out the reverse. Measure the height of the bottom edge of the frame (portrait orientation). Divide that into three and you have your increments for the top and bottom line of nails (1).

2. Working now on the front side of the frame, I like to put a line of tape along the sides I'm working on so the pencil marks are nice and obvious. Working on the bottom side of the frame, measure and mark the one third and two thirds distance from the bottom of the frame at the right, centre and left of the frame (2). Draw a line at these marks along the length of the side of the frame. Do the same from the top edge.

3. Starting 1cm (⅜in) in from the side of the frame, put a mark on the top drawn line every 1cm (⅜in) along the frame (3). On the bottom line, start 1.5cm (⅝in) in from the opening of the frame, and put a mark every 1cm (⅜in). Do the same on the bottom side of the frame.

4. Now you can grab your nails and hammer, and hammer a nail into each mark on the top and bottom lines, at the top and bottom of the frame (4). The nails should be embedded to a depth of at least 1.5cm (⅝in), or until they are really firm in the frame (5). Wiggle room is a bad thing!

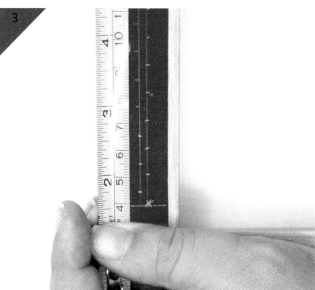

If your frame is splitting or the nails seem to be missing the mark, pre-drilling a starter hole for each mark, using either a cordless drill or a nail punch, might help.

Warping Your Loom

Here is the first bit of technical terminology for your weaving adventure: The Warp. The warp is the fibre stretched in place vertically on a loom, which you will then weave onto. Basically it means the up and down strings, or warp strings, that you will go over and under and round and round to make your weaving.

The pieces you'll see in this book all use the same type of warp thread, which is a thin 0.5mm non-stretchy cotton thread. There are lots of thread options out there, with differing thicknesses and colours available. I use this one as it can be doubled up without adding bulk to the loom, and is excellent for use in pieces that need fine details like curves and lettering. Different colours can be fun to experiment with, especially on texture pieces where you might use a technique like diamond twill (see *Diamond Twill*) so that those warp strings peek through and pop with a little contrast colour.

YOU WILL NEED

› Your loom

› Cotton warp thread, approx 5–10g (⅛–¼oz) per weaving, I use 0.5mm diameter cotton warp thread

› Scissors

› Shed stick – a stick of balsa wood, 12.5mm (½in), rectangular, and at least 10cm (4in) wider than the width of your loom

› A piece of standard printer paper the width of your loom

HOW TIGHT?

Well that's a matter of preference. Super tight means the frame will be under stress, it might be hard to pass a needle through, and your project could shrink a little when it comes off the loom. Too saggy and it'll be hard to weave, and it could make your piece wobbly when it's hung. Here is the trick: you need to keep the string the same tension across the whole expanse of the frame. It is a technique that takes practice to know when it's right, but here are my top tips:

> Don't stop and start when warping. Keep the up and down motion going, paying attention to how strongly you're pulling the thread. Uniformity is the key.

> Before you tie off at the end, run your fingers across the strings like a guitar. You want to be able to thrum your fingers across and feel the same tension across all the strings (5).

> If you have some saggy strings, manually tighten them by pulling them tighter as they move to the right, but beware you don't make them tighter than the rest.

SINGLE STRING WARPING

1. Tie a shallow loop knot (as shown) into the end of your warp thread and secure the string to the first nail at the bottom left of the frame (1).

2. With your right hand guiding the cotton and your left pulling it off the ball, run the string up to the top left nail, across to the staggered nail below and back down to the nail second from the left (2).

3. Keep the tension in the string by using your left hand to evenly loop the cotton around each nail. At approximately a third of the way across the loom, wind a loop of the cotton around two nails to create a lock for the tension in the previous warp strings (3).

4. Continue warping the loom in the up and down 'S' pattern (4).

5. Once you get to the end of the loom, count your pairs of strings. At the end of a weave, you'll tie the bottom warp threads together; the one that went up to the neighbouring thread that went down. They will make a single knot to pair the two threads together. At the top of the loom when you string it onto a hanging rod, that pair will make one loop around the hanger, and it will be tied to the next 'pair' of threads. You're aiming to have matching pairs all the way along so they each have a neighbour to tie off to. Simply put, make sure when you warp, you warp in sets of four threads. Once you have an even number, tie a loop knot in the cotton where the string should end and loop it over the last nail.

6. Once tied off, thread your shed stick over and under each alternative string until it is centred across the loom. The shed stick should overhang your loom by at least 5cm (2in) each side (6).

7. Cut a strip of paper a few centimetres wider than your weaving, and 4cm (1½in) high. This is called a warp spacer. Weave it over and under every few warp strings and push it right to the bottom of the frame so it sits right on the bottom (7). This is the point on your loom that your first row of tabby will start (see *Starting a Weave with Tabby*), so if you're using a template it should be positioned to line up with your warp spacer.

DOUBLE STRING WARPING

Follow the warping steps above, and when you come to the bottom right-hand nail on the frame, make your loop knot but instead of cutting the thread, swing back up and continue warping a second layer, right to left, over the same nails. When threading in your shed stick, each doubled vertical string will be treated as a single string. In other words, don't split them. Each project in this book will indicate whether you'll need a single or double warped loom for the piece.

If you're fiddling with the tension,
start again. You'll be more frustrated
if you persevere and then scrap
it four hours in, trust me.

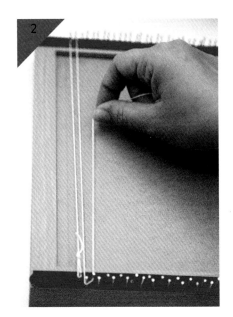

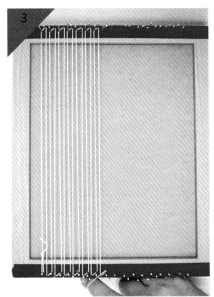

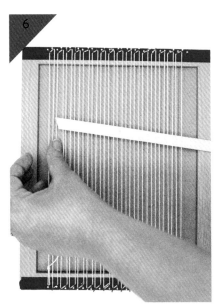

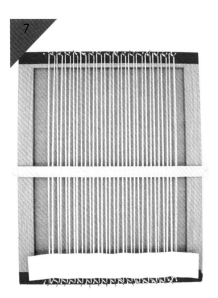

Choosing Your Yarn

Now we get to the fun part. And I'm going to be straight with you – it's a process that's as fun as you make it. Sure, there are weavers that are dedicated to only using organic wool. Vegan wool is a thing too. Some are passionate about a particular colour scheme and won't stray far from it. And some just want to use it all. Hi – that's me. I happily source colourful acrylic yarn from the discount store, and then hit up my wonderful independent yarn store for some hand-spun or hand-dyed loveliness. I find amazing roving on Etsy, and I go to the big national craft stores and fill up on everything when they have a good sale.

Lace ⟶ Roving

In my books, every yarn has a place if you love it and have a use for it, so here is a bit of a breakdown of what I've learned and a summary of the types of yarn I've used in this book. It is by no means a comprehensive list – I'm not a wool expert, and you don't really need to know the technical aspects such as needle size, ply, or tension swatches for this type of weaving – but here is a little general overview of what's what, and how it can be used.

WEIGHT

The Craft Yarn Council has developed official standards for the sizing of yarns, but what one spinner calls 'chunky' yarn might not be the same as what a woollen mill on the other side of the world calls it. Weight isn't a huge factor when it comes to weaving, as techniques such as weft-facing weaving (see *Weft-facing Weaving*) accommodates chunkier yarns, or triple threading finer yarns can be a little shortcut to incorporate any type of yarn that you like into your piece. However, here is a basic guide to yarn weights.

CATEGORY	Lace	Superfine	Fine	Light	Medium	Bulky	Super Bulky	Jumbo
TYPES OF YARNS	Fingering, Crochet thread	Sock, Fingering, Baby	Sport, Baby	DK, Light, Worsted	Worsted, Afghan, Aran	Chunky, Craft, Rug	Super bulky, Roving	Jumbo, Roving
METRIC NEEDLE SIZE	1.5–2.25mm	2.25–3.25mm	3.25–3.75mm	3.75–4.5mm	4.5–5.5mm	5.5–8mm	8–12.75mm	12.75 and larger
US NEEDLE SIZE	000–1	1–3	3–5	5–7	7–9	9–11	11–17	17 and larger
	This group of yarns are great for fine detail in weavings like tassels, shapes and faces, but can be time consuming if you're looking to weave a large area. If using with other types of yarns, consider doubling or tripling the threads on the needle to keep the right shape on the loom.			Easily found in an array of colours, these sizes are basically the standard weight of yarn. They are great for weaving shapes and getting consistent tension on the weave. Because they are on the fine side, it will take time to build up in large areas of your weaving. Also, these are the go-to sizes for rya knots because you can add or take away strands from each bunch easily to fit the piece.		Amazing for texture, solid shapes, and twill patterns. Make quick work of backgrounds. It's common for chunky to be 1 ply, meaning one thick strand of wool, so be careful as it can tease apart easily if you're using it for things like rya knots etc. The chunkier the yarn, the more blocky the shape, so if you're going for curves, avoid the chunkies. If you're doing hair or any type of texture though, these are for you.		Fun zone! Roving can make a real statement in a piece. Soumak (see *Soumak*) is a show stopper on textured pieces and roving is a must for these.

FIBRES AND EFFECTS

There are countless types of fibre out there, in myriad blends and styles. Here is a rundown of some materials you'll see in the projects in this book.

Wool (100% wool, alpaca wool, merino etc)	Ok, so I think we all know wool. Popular, natural, comes from animals. Wool is available in a range of colours and weights. Alpaca and merino are super soft and merino is available from fine to roving. They're more expensive than their man-made counterparts but are lovely to work with and make your pieces dreamy soft.
Cotton	Cotton yarns come in a huge range of colours and blends, but beware of weaving large areas with them as they don't have the stretch of wool and can turn your weaving into an hourglass shape. *However,* get your hands on some chunky cotton fibre, use it as a rya knot, brush the ends out and the fibres are amazing!
Acrylic	A synthetic fibre that is cheap and available in tons of colours. This yarn sometimes has a sheen to it, so be mindful if you're mixing it with natural fibres.
Mohair	A great way to add texture to a piece, particularly hair to a pet or person portrait. Avoid these yarns if you're doing an intricate pattern like a twill or soumak, as the shapes will be lost in the fibre.
Bouclé	A type of spun yarn that is great for adding some fluff to texture pieces and fuzz to fur portraits.
Hand-painted/hand-dyed yarn	There are a wealth of wonderful creatives out there who put their hearts into dying yarn. From subtle colour washes to in-your-face colour explosions, these are great to play with.
Roving	Roving is that incredible fluffy thick stuff that you see in so many textural weavings. Sometimes referred to as spinning fibre or top, it is wool fibre that has been processed, carded, but not yet spun into yarn. Available in all sorts of colours and differing microns, which measure the thickness of each individual fibre strand. The smaller the micron number, the better quality the fibre.

Creating a Template

The pieces you're going to make in this book all work off templates, and the loom you have made will work hand-in-hand to help you achieve weaving glory by unleashing your own creativity. We're going to learn how to create a few different types of templates for you to use and adapt to your own style. The first project in this book has a template available in the back (see *Templates*) so we can figure out the process together. After that, you'll take over as creative director. With the loom you've made, the dimensions you have to play with are 50cm (20in) long and 39cm (15¼in) wide, plus the fringe length. Pieces can be shorter or narrower so it's up to you how you adapt your templates to fit into that area.

HAND-DRAWN TEMPLATE

All you need is a sheet or two of A3 paper (or some A4 sheets taped together) and your imagination. And a pencil. And maybe an eraser. But that's about it. Be sure to leave a gap of 8cm (3¼in) or so at the top of your loom, so you have room to thread a hanging rod, and about 4cm (1½in) at the bottom for the paper warp spacer to slide in. Other than that, start sketching away with your designs.

LOW-TECH 1:1 RATIO PICTURE TEMPLATE

If your chosen image is the right size for your loom, you can use the tried and trusted tracing paper method to transfer it to paper. Just leave at least an 8cm (3¼in) gap at the top of your loom, and about 4cm (1½in) at the bottom.

Tape the image to a window, lay a sheet of paper over it and begin tracing the shapes of your subject in pencil. Outline the areas for the different yarn colours, making a simple line drawing of the subject.

Once you're happy with your tracing, you can go over the primary lines with a felt-tip pen so they stand out behind the warp strings. You can even colour in some areas to see what works for your design before you get started on the loom.

MID-TECH PHOTO TEMPLATE

There is some tech involved here, but nothing outside the realms of Microsoft Excel and using a printer. I'm assuming you are starting with a digital photo on your computer, and we're not going all the way back to physical photographs.

Open Microsoft Excel and 'Insert' the picture into a blank worksheet. Using the picture tools, you can crop out the unnecessary background and re-centre the image to how you want it to appear on your loom. Next resize the image to fit the dimensions of the weaving area of your loom. In the colour menu you can choose to dial down the colour saturation so you don't use your entire week's wages on computer ink. Select 'Print', set the margins to narrow, and print out your image. Trim off half the borders so you can tape the pieces together, and then using a felt-tip pen, start marking in the main shapes of the image. These pen marks will be the template you weave to, so be mindful to edit out any unnecessary detail that may cause you to cry in frustration later. Things like facial features can be drawn in but will be woven over with the skin tone, in which case you'll use the template as a guide to embroider those details back in.

HI-TECH PHOTO TEMPLATE

If you have a tablet, there are lots of apps to help with sketching from a photo, such as Adobe Draw or Autodesk Sketchbook Pro. Find one that lets you use layers. This will allow you to import a picture, make it opaque and add a new drawing layer over the top. Then you can simply trace the outlines on the top layer, and when the time comes, fade the picture layer right out to zero. Magic. You are then left with a sketch to follow, and can resize it to your loom using the mid-tech poster printing method.

Using Your Template

Exactly why am I double stringing this loom, and how on earth am I supposed to use it?! Let's chat. If tabby (see *Starting a Weave with Tabby*) is the basis to most of the shapes you'll be weaving, double stringing your loom is the next step to kick the shapes into high gear. I'm going to break down how to use the template and the double stringing that will be used in almost every piece in this book.

HOW IT WORKS

› After placing your template on the backboard of the loom, double string your loom (see *Warping Your Loom:Double String Warping*), making sure that the image is centred to your loom both vertically and horizontally, and that the threads are coupled together. You want to be able to tie them off in pairs when you're done (1).

› Once you have your anchoring tabby (see *Starting a Weave with Tabby*) and rya fringe (see *Rya Knots*) in place at the bottom of the loom, you can start working to the template. Think of the way you weave as working with house bricks: you can build a straight vertical line. Cool. You can build a curve that falls away from the line. Tick. But an overhang? You'll need support. It's the same with weaving shapes. You always want some support in place below before you start pushing over the top.

› The first section you need to weave is the support line, weaving tabby over and under each column of warp strings until the template demands a change. As it slowly steps away, each row will take half steps, using the double strings to follow that change. Sometimes the template will need a large change in shape, and you'll find yourself stepping back two, three or four warp threads at a time, but keep going until that section requires an overhang (2).

› At the point of the overhang, the new section will need to catch up and provide the support. Weave up the line with the new yarn (3), sliding in to those half-strung steps, trying to marry them neatly side by side, not pulling them apart. This is where your tension and bubbling are key (see *Starting a Weave with Tabby*), giving the yarn enough room to sit comfortably on the line. Just like last time, continue upwards until the change in yarn is required, and the other side will play catch up (4).

› When weaving complex shapes with templates, you'll likely have three or four different sections going at once, changing the support section every few rows. Keeping your template firm and fixed in the frame means that you don't need to guess what change is next, you can just follow the shape.

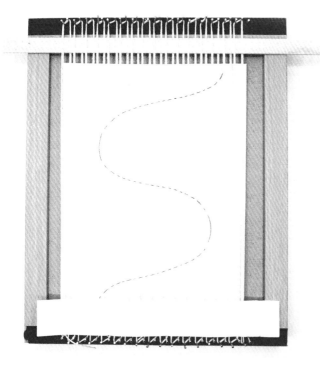

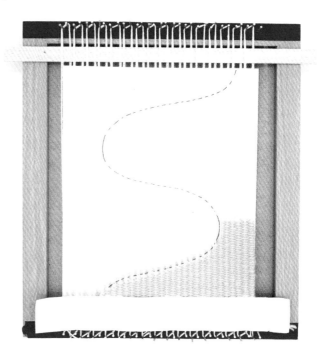

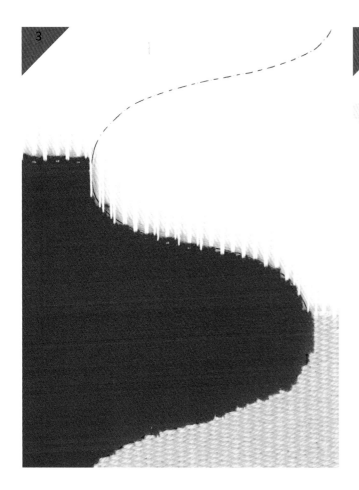

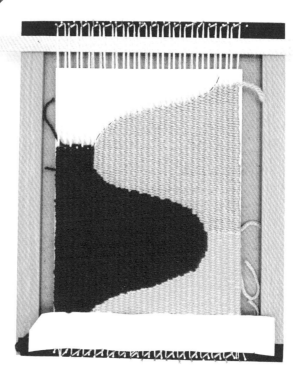

Starting a Weave with Tabby

Your loom is warped. Your yarn is waiting. Let's get started! This technique is the building block of any piece that has a rya fringe (see *Rya Knots*), so we'll start off laying the base layer. Bear in mind that this tabby technique is the bread and butter of any piece, so get it right and you'll be cruising.

YOU WILL NEED

> A warped loom

> Yarn, generally light- to medium-weight

> Scissors

> Tapestry needle, I prefer metal over plastic

> A shed stick

> A beater (when I started an ordinary kitchen fork worked just fine)

1. Cut a length of the yarn you will be using for the fringe that is a generous six times the width of your frame and thread it into your tapestry needle.

2. With your shed stick in the middle field of the loom, turn it to the narrow side, creating an open space that pushes every second warp thread up and the alternating threads down. Slide your needle through this gap from left to right, keeping a 5cm (2in) tail of yarn at the end. As it is in the open space of the shed stick gap, it will slide through easily – think of this as the express lane of unders and overs. Don't pull it tight, just let it lie in its natural tension (1). Roll the shed stick flat again, to close the gap.

3. Next use your needle to go under and over the threads in the opposite direction and sequence, aiming 10–15cm (4–6in) above the bottom row in an arc shape. When your needle is back to the left of the loom, hold the last warp thread together with the end of the yarn on the previous row and pull through your excess yarn, keeping it in a smooth arc shape (2).

4. Using your beater and working in quarters, push the centre of the arc down to the bottom row. Then push the front quarter down, then the third quarter (3). Once the three points are touching the bottom row, work your way along to flatten the entire arc to the bottom row (4). This is called 'bubbling' and will ensure that the tension of the weaving is uniform. The paper spacer at the bottom of your loom will help keep that first row straight. Your goal is to push the rows together so there are no warp threads visible, using the same pressure for each row, so the density is consistent throughout.

5. Continue this tabby weave up and up by rolling that shed stick to its 'open' position, passing left to right, bubbling and beating to the previous row, rolling the shed stick closed, then picking under and over in the opposite direction (5), until you have 6–8 rows to anchor your weaving. If you run out of yarn, cut another length, pushing the tails to the back (this will make it easier to weave them in at the end) and continuing on the same over under sequence of that line.

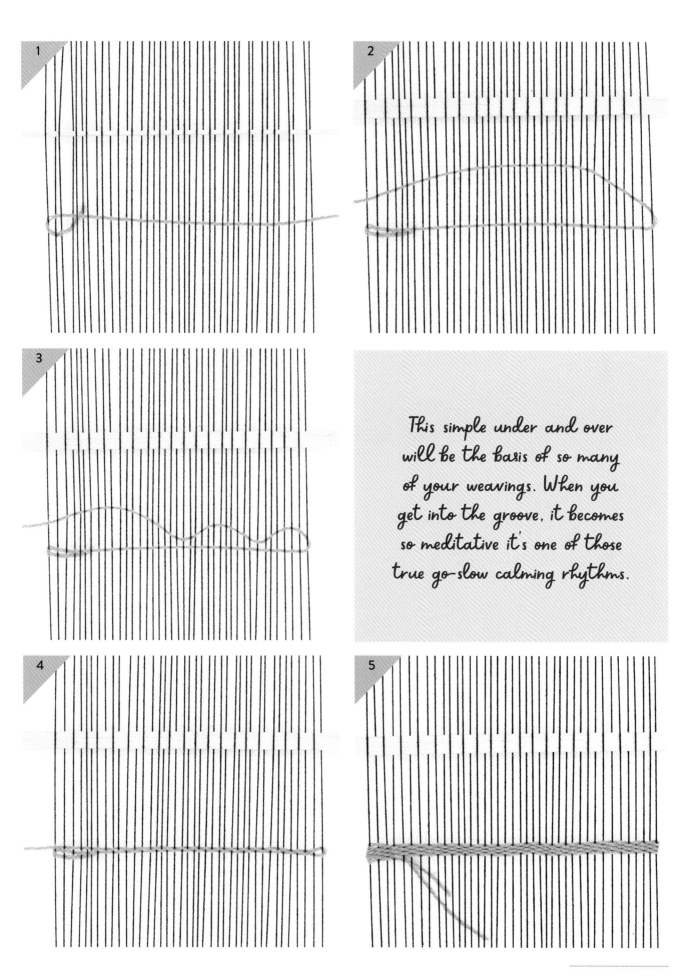

This simple under and over will be the basis of so many of your weavings. When you get into the groove, it becomes so meditative it's one of those true go-slow calming rhythms.

Rya Knots

Those fringy bottom bits of a weave have a name: they are rya knots, or rya loops, and they're kind of like tassels anchored within a weaving. They can be as long or short as you want, and can be used in the body of a weaving to add texture and movement too. You can cut your rya lengths freestyle using your hand to loop the yarn around before cutting it, but I like the consistency of using a guide.

YOU WILL NEED

> A warped loom with 6–8 tabby rows as a base (see *Starting a Weave with Tabby*)

> Yarn, generally light- to medium-weight

> Scissors

> A piece of rigid cardboard 15 x 10cm (6 x 4in)

1. For the fringes in this book I've used a 10cm (4in) rya guide made from a piece of rigid cardboard. This will make a consistent fringe about 4.5cm (1¾in) in length. If want your fringe longer, bear in mind the yarn will need to be double the length of the fringe because it twists up around the strings. Wind the yarn 20–30 times around the guide, paying attention to the tension (1). The tighter the yarn is wound, the shorter the fringe will be.

2. Cut the yarn from the guide and lay the strands flat on your workspace. The number of strands you need for each knot will depend on the thickness of your yarn. Start with five or six strands – you can add or subtract from there.

3. Gather the strands so one set of ends are all level and laying flat. Find the middle of the bunch – that is the section you want to be at the front of the loom – and hold it above the warp strings at the bottom left of your frame (2).

4. Using your left hand, guide the left side of the bunch behind the loom around and through to the front, below the centre of the bunch

(3). Pull all the tails of the left side bunch through. Your right hand should be keeping the right-hand side in place and laying straight. Now guide the right side of the bunch around the second warp thread, behind the loom and back through the centre of the first warp thread pair (4). Pull the right-hand tails gently into place, they should be a similar length to the left-hand side. If it's way off, loosen the knot by pulling the front of the bunch out from the loom a little and re-jig the levels. Fair warning, it's hard to keep the front of the knot tidy once you start messing with it, if so unwind it and start again.

5. Repeat this process around strings 3 and 4 for the next rya knot, and review how they look together. The goal is to not see any of the tabby line at the bottom from between the rya, but not have them bulging into each other, throwing out the tension. Add or remove strands from the rya bunches until you have a nice straight uniform row of rya all the way to the end (5). If in doubt, be more generous – you don't want to stinge on the fringe!

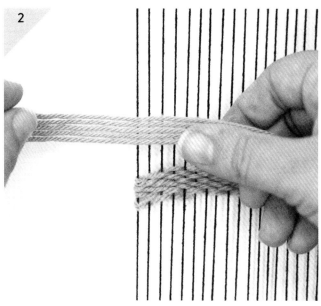

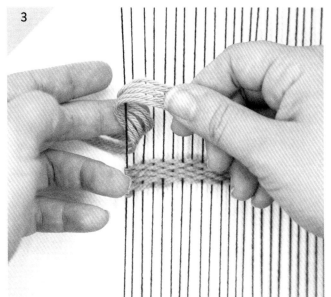

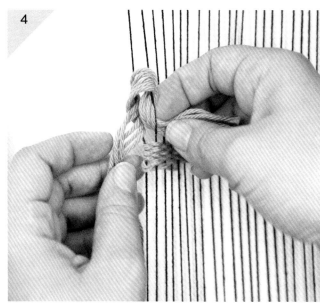

Leave trimming your rya until your weaving is off the loom and hung on its rod to avoid exacerbating any wonkiness in the piece with a wonky rya fringe.

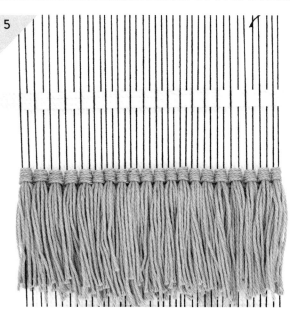

Weft-facing Weaving

If you just can't resist those chunky yarns, be warned – they can turn your straight edges into a wobbly mess. Now we could go down the technical rabbit hole of ends-per-inch and yarn density, but I'll just say this: in most weaves you aim to hide the warp threads behind your yarn, but sometimes the chunky stuff not only shows too much of the warp threads, but also throws off the shape of your weave. If this is the case, here is a technique for you.

YOU WILL NEED

› A warped loom
› Chunky yarn
› Scissors
› Tapestry needle
› Beater
› Shed stick

1. Thread a long strand of your chunky yarn onto your tapestry needle and starting at the left side of your loom, bring the yarn under the first warp thread and over the second and third (1).

2. Continue along the row using this 2–1 method. Have a look at the warp threads. Are they still nice and straight vertically? Are some of them bending out to accommodate the yarn? If it looks to be a tight squeeze, adapt the pattern to a 3–1 sequence.

3. On your next row, you want to make sure you go over the previous row's unders, but instead of a 2–1 sequence, change it up between 2 overs and an under, 3 overs and an under and maybe even some single under overs. This gives a nice textured look with the randomness that shows it isn't a traditional twill technique (2 & 3).

4. Personally, I like a textured look so I don't aim to replicate the row sequences. I like to start choosing random intervals for a 2–1, maybe a few 3–1, heck, maybe a 4–1 to keep the pattern scattered and not obvious (4). This is a really nice technique to give a little added texture to portraits for things like jumpers, hair, clouds etc because it looks bubbly, textured and raised. Step back from the work every now and then to check for patterns that have formed in the attempt at randomness.

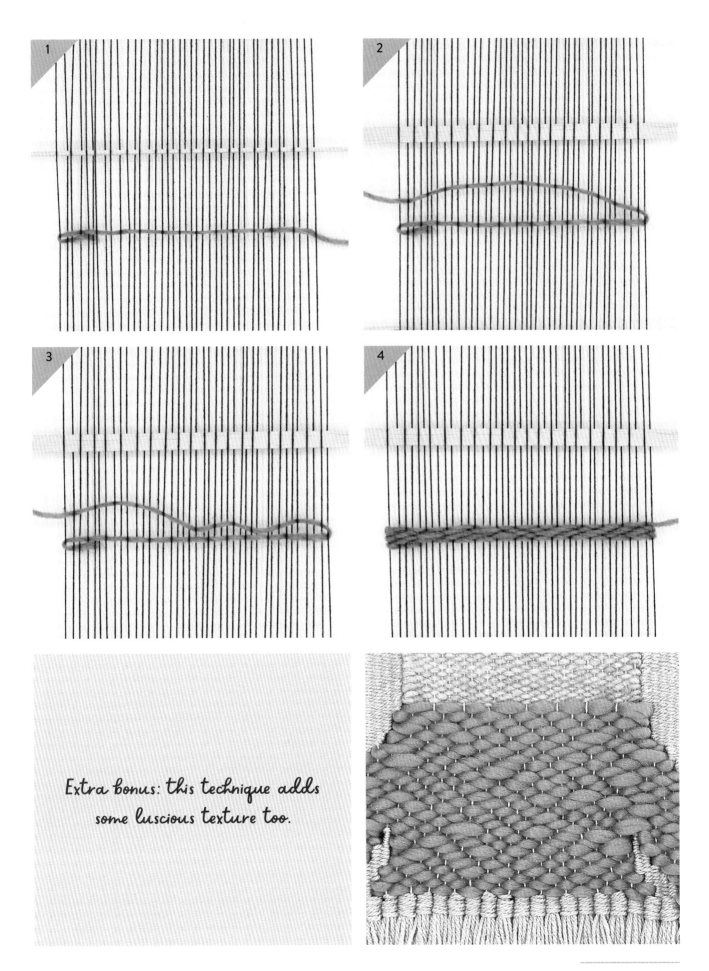

Extra bonus: this technique adds some luscious texture too.

Soumak

This one is a stunner, and a weaver's favourite on textured pieces. Whether you're using wool roving (that amazing fluffy stuff that is actually wool *before* it has been spun into yarn) or plain yarn, soumak can be as simple or as statement as you want it. This technique is for texture lovers and can be done in a straight line, or to sit along a curve, or to fill in a blank space. So versatile and always a winner.

FISHTAIL SOUMAK USING ROVING

YOU WILL NEED

> A warped loom with 6–8 tabby rows as a base (see *Starting a Weave with Tabby*)

> A length of roving twice as long as the row you want to weave

> Scissors

1. The first thing to do is to gently run the length of roving through your hands (1). As it is unspun, you just want to smooth out the length and tease off any little fluffy bits off from the main length. It will take a length around one and a half times the length of the row you want to weave to fill it using the soumak technique.

2. Starting on the left side of your loom, bring your roving over three warp threads, leaving a short tail (about 4cm/1½in) hanging out to the left. At the third string, bring the roving around, down, and back through, finishing with your roving at the front again (2). Just like with the warp-facing weave (see *Warp-facing Weaving*), have a look at how the warp threads are holding up. If your roving is looking a little too chunky, go to a 4–1 sequence. If it's a bit barren, go 2–1.

3. Bring your roving over the next three warp threads from there and again go around, under and through (3). Repeat this pattern until you have filled your row or section. There's your first soumak row (4).

4. For the braided look, gather another length of roving and starting again from the left, at the fourth string in, wind the roving around, up and through, finishing with your roving at the front again (5).

5. Continue the sequence of over three warp threads, around, up and out, tucking them gently into the spaces of the lower braid to enhance the fishtail look (6).

6. Tuck the ends in behind the loom into a few warp threads at once.

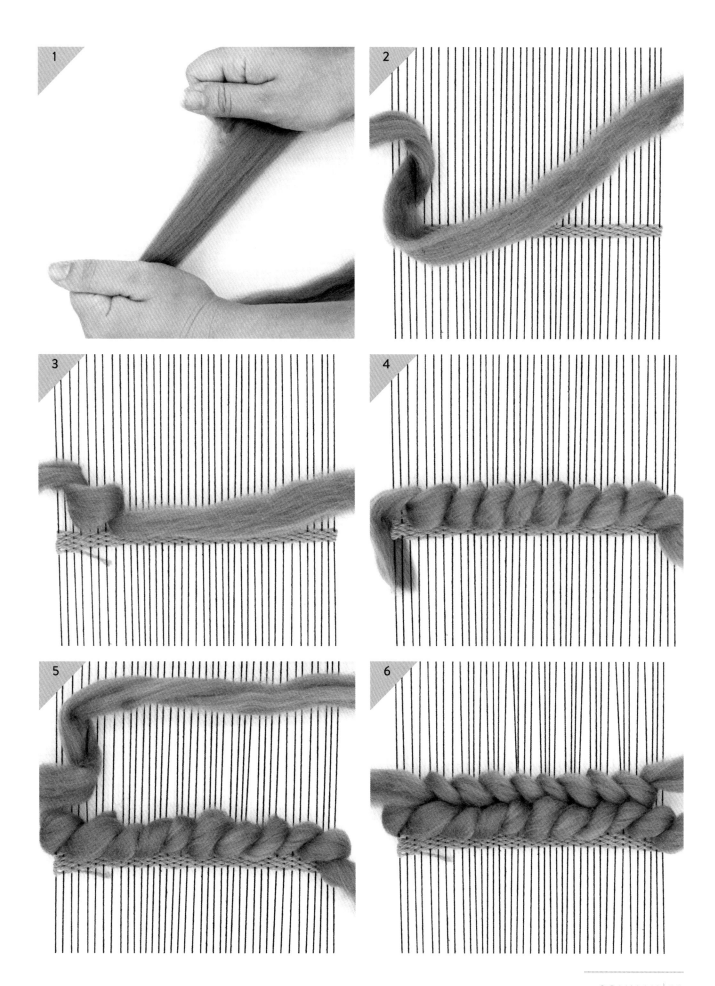

SOUMAK USING MULTIPLE YARN THREADS

If you can't get your hands on any roving, or want a chunky braid in a different colour, you can always just use various strands of yarn for a chunky multi-texture soumak braid. Simply cut a length of yarn around one and a half times the length of the row you want to weave, and cut some more yarns to the same length. If the multiple strands feel a bit too much to handle while you're working with them, tie a loose knot in the end of the yarn you're weaving with, so they are all bound together, and use that as your end.

Depending on how many yarns, use your judgement on the sequence they need. Over two warp threads and under and around one, perhaps over three warp threads, perhaps over four.

When finished, weave the ends into the back of the weave, into skipped warp threads or into the back of the stitches.

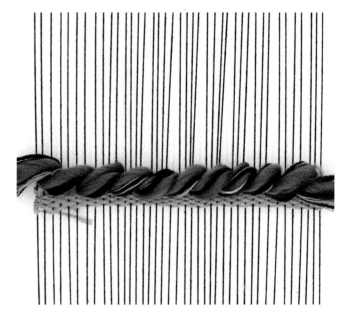

If you're going to layer soumak braids one on top of the other, slide a double row of basic under-and-over tabby weaving between them to keep them secure.

Diamond Twill

Here it is... the show-stopper of techniques, the one that seems way too complicated, the one that everyone will admire. The one you're going to learn how to *nail*. It's basically about constructing rows of triangles – there are only two steps involved but keep a sharp eye because detail is the key here.

YOU WILL NEED

> A warped loom
> Selected yarn, chunky works great with this style
> Tapestry needle
> Beater
> Scissors

1. Count five warp strings in from the left-hand side of your weave, and weave your first over row over the sixth (1). Go under another five, over the sixth. That's the basis of starting this pattern: 5–1–5–1... Every three rows it will revert to this pattern. Easy.

2. For your second row, going back in the opposite direction, you want to weave over each thread that is above either side of the single overs on the first line (2). You will see a pattern developing of over one, under one, over one, under three: 1–3–1–3. Just like with your tabby, arch your row, bubble it and beat it flat (see *Starting a Weave with Tabby*).

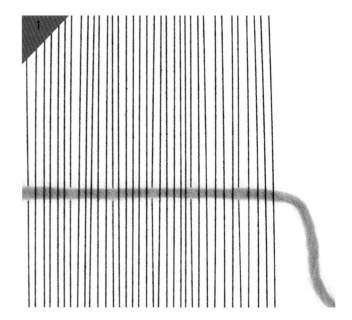

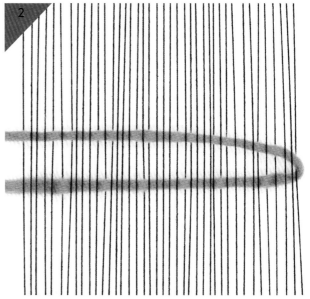

3. You can see from the first two rows the diamond pattern already starting to emerge: the base then two steps either side (3). For your third row, you will be adding another step out to form the diamonds. Bring your thread around and under the first warp thread, over the second, under the third and over the fourth. That fourth step over should create a line diagonally down to the first row's first over. Now go under three, over one, under one, over one and you will start seeing a pattern of the 1–3–1–3 variety again (4).

4. Happy days! We are at the end and also the start. You should be able to see the shape of the triangles forming. For the fourth row, you revert back to the 5–1–5–1 sequence and go over the warp thread that sits above the over/under/over pairs in the previous row, and tops off the triangles.

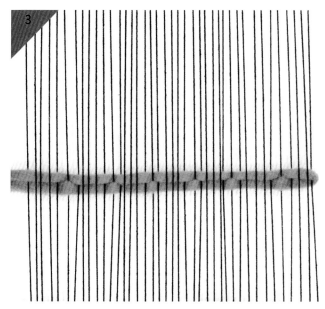

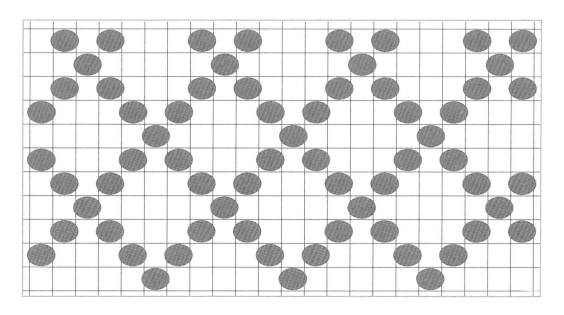

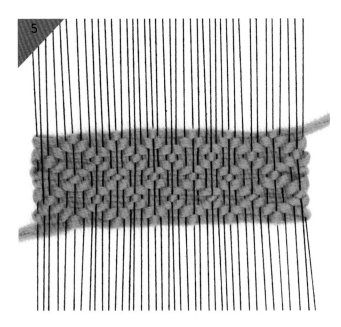

The chunkier your yarn, the easier it is to spot the sequences forming, and the less likely it is that the diamonds will squish in on themselves when your work comes off the loom.

5. Now it's time to close out the diamond, and you do this by simply repeating the same steps, just stepped over a few warp threads, because the bottom right of every diamond is the top left of another. Your thread should be over the left-hand side of the loom after the fourth row. Bring it over the top of the first two threads and under the third. Over the fourth, under three, over one, under one, over one, under three. Here is the 1–3–1–3 sequence again.

6. For the sixth row, have a look at the diamond formed over the right-hand side. Count it up and see which threads need to come next to construct the next step. It will be the 1–3 1–3 sequence again.

7. Close out the seventh row with the 5–1–5–1 sequence and follow the pattern as high as you desire (5). If you need to thread in a new length of yarn during this sequence, be sure to secure the loose ends on the back side of the loom, tucked into the back of one of the overs of the diamond pattern so the pattern isn't interrupted.

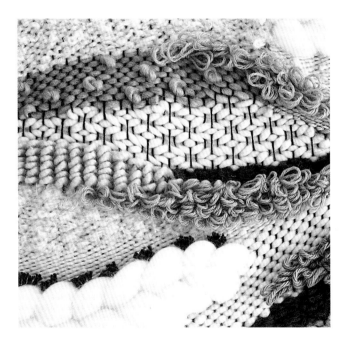

Pile Weaving

So you say you like texture? Well welcome to pile weaving, your new best friend. This technique is perfect for filling in spaces with some texture, doing a large strong band of 'floof' through a piece, or even giving a beard or a hairstyle some funky texture in a portrait. Grab a couple of knitting needles, pencils, or the very steady and patient fingers of a friend, and let's get going.

YOU WILL NEED

> A warped loom
> Selected yarn – chunky ones work great with this style
> Tapestry needle
> Two or more knitting needles – I use 7.5mm (US11), or two pencils also work
> Beater
> Shed stick
> Scissors

1. With your shed stick in place, start from the right side of the loom to weave a row of tabby (see *Starting a Weave with Tabby*), going in the opposite up and down pattern to the shed stick (1).

2. For the next row, open the shed stick and pass the thread along the open path, making sure to set it in an arch for bubbling (2).

3. From the left side of the row, pick up the first 'over', pull it gently out from the loom (making sure to pull it from the side of the loose yarn for slack, not the woven side), poke the tip of the knitting needle down through the gap, and gently push the knitting needle forward to the next stitch. Continue along the row pulling out each over stitch gently using the excess yarn to the right for the slack, and always going in the same 'poke the top and through' direction (3). Once you have the row onto the needle, pull it down to sit against the first row of basic under-and-over tabby weaving and keep the knitting needle in place.

4. For the next row, weave a row of tabby in the alternative pattern of the shed stick again and beat it down onto the knitting needle row (4).

5. Open the shed stick again, arch a row of tabby in before winding it onto another needle, using the same 'poke the top and through' technique as the first row, and finishing with another row of tabby above (5).

6. Gently remove the knitting needles and the pile should stay in place (6). Take your beater and gently push the rows together, making sure not to pull the pile loops out of alignment.

7. Stack row upon row of tabby/pile up as far as you'd like (7).

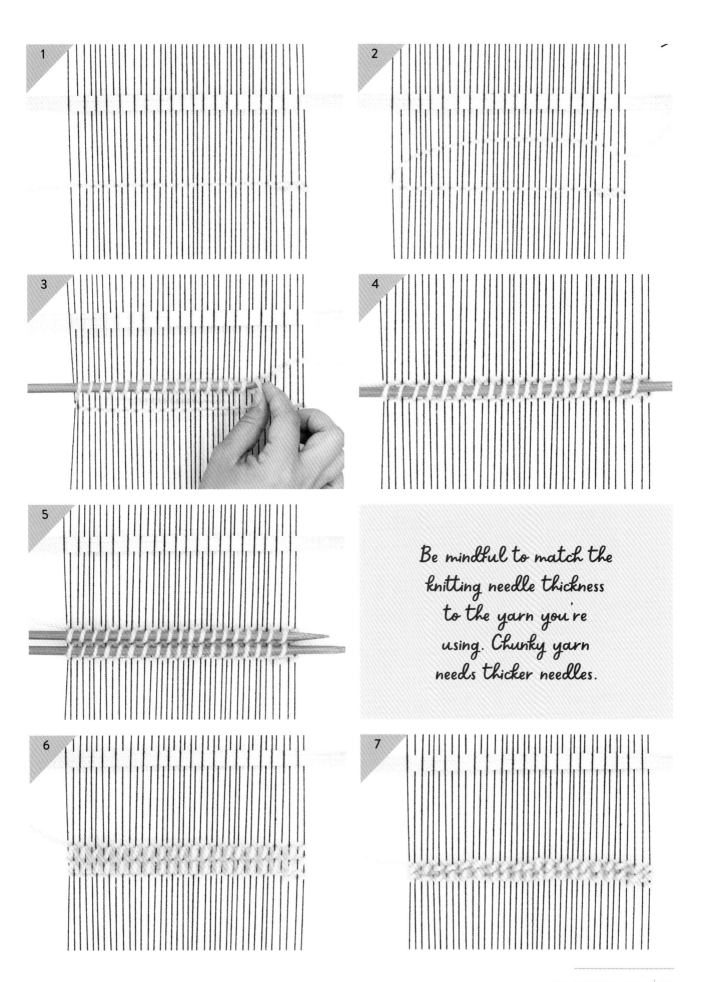

Be mindful to match the knitting needle thickness to the yarn you're using. Chunky yarn needs thicker needles.

Overweaving

I'll be honest, I haven't seen this around as a 'technique' so I kind of made up the name. Sounds good, right? This technique will be a main part of portraits, as it is the hair technique. Any area of overweaving needs to be supported by a base of tabby in the general hair colour, and overweaving will be the last step you complete before taking the weaving off the loom.

YOU WILL NEED

› Your portrait weave completed using the template

› Three gradients of a hair tone

› A marker pen

› Scissors

› Tapestry needle

1. Once you've completed your portrait weave, and the hair section is filled with a base of tabby weave (see *Starting a Weave with Tabby*), lift out the backing from your frame and weave in all the yarn ends. (I suggest you listen to Pink Floyd as you work – staring into the Dark Side of the Loom while weaving in ends is the worst.)

2. Using your template as a guide to the direction of the hair, mark up the weave with a marker pen, indicating where the hair flows (1).

3. Thread the darkest gradient yarn onto the needle and weave along the lines you've just drawn (2). Keep as much of the yarn on the front of the loom, by weaving like a running stitch – anchoring the thread behind one row of the tabby before coming to the front of the loom and weaving a line with the yarn (3). Try to work your way across the shape from one side to the other so there is less yarn making trails behind the weave. As you overweave contours and corners, keep the length of your sections to a maximum of 4–5cm (1½–2in), shortening that as you curve around corners.

4. Once the darkest layer has been put down, tuck in the ends behind the weave so there isn't a tangled mess back there. Then, start filling in with the mid-colour (4). This will generally be the dominant hair colour, as the lightest will be used as a highlight. Continue filling in the hair across the shape, overweaving in the natural shape and direction of the hair, and leaving sections for the highlight colour.

5. The final colour will highlight the crown of the head, main sections of movement in the hair and the lightest pieces around the face.

1

When you're doing your template, think about how the hair falls and what parts hit the light and where the shadows are. Look at artists' illustrations for guidance.

2

3

Tension is important when overweaving because if the yarn is pulled too tight, the flat tabby weave sections around the overweaving will be pulled out of shape.

4

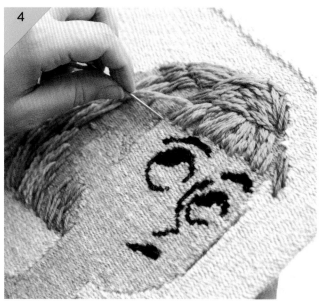

Bobbles

Welcome to another simple technique to add some texture and raised areas to a portrait or textured weaving. These little guys look great when you're using a nice chunky yarn, and if you can tie your shoes, then you can do this technique.

YOU WILL NEED

› A warped loom
› Selected yarn, chunky works great with this style
› Tapestry needle
› Beater
› Shed Stick
› Scissors

1. Start by weaving a line of simple tabby (see *Starting a Weave with Tabby*) at the bottom of your shape, using the chunky yarn (1).

2. On the second row back the other way, weave a quarter of the way along the line, and pull until the yarn is all the way through. Tie a simple overhand knot in the yarn right down at the face of the weaving. Keep it loose so it stands out (2).

3. Continue following the under over sequence for the rest of the row. On the third row, tabby across a third of the row, tie another overhand knot in the yarn so it sits right on the face of the weave, and complete the rest of the row (3).

4. You can use this simple technique to add a few bobbles in here and there (4), or to add a full cluster of texture in areas of your weaving. Both random placement and organised plotted points of these little balls of fun look great.

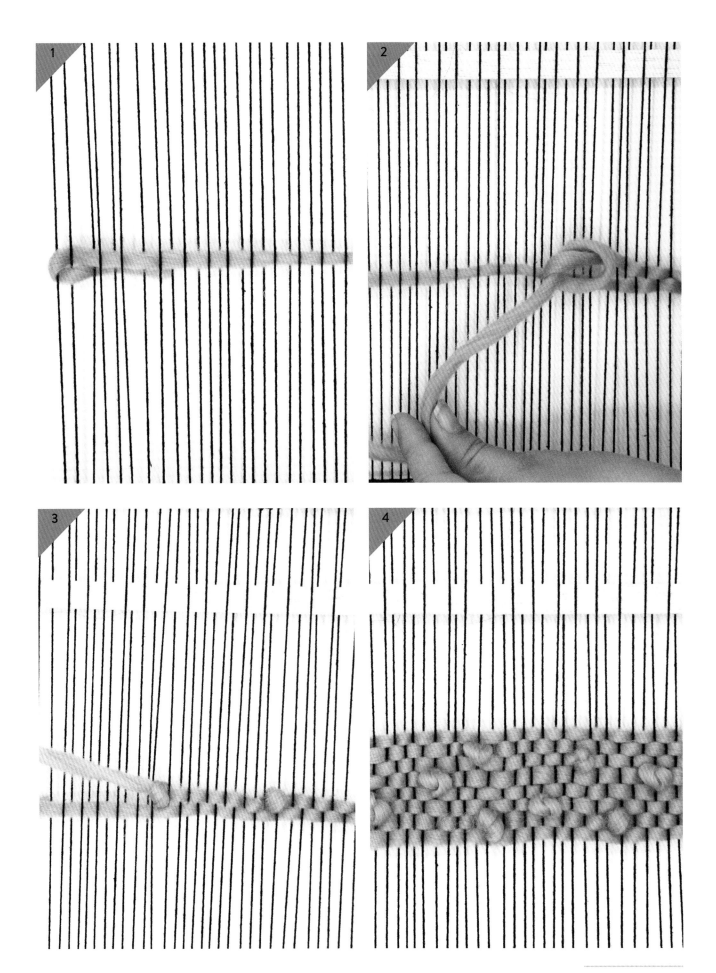

Inverted and Continuous Rya

You've met rya. She's the gal that hangs around at the bottom of your weave, making that slick-looking fringe. Here are two variations on the theme that will serve you well when adding some dimension to your creations, particularly in textured weaves and portraits.

YOU WILL NEED

> A warped loom

> Your yarn of choice

> A piece of rigid cardboard 15 x 10cm (6 x 4in)

> Scissors

> Shed stick

> Beater

If you are adding these to a double-stringed loom, place them across a full span of warp thread. If you try to squeeze them in the half steps of the warp, it will throw the straight sides out.

INVERTED RYA

You will absolutely recognise this one. It is your standard rya knot (see *Rya Knots*), but upside down.

1. Like any standard rya row, you need a supporting tabby row underneath first (see *Starting a Weave with Tabby*), preferably in the same colour as your knots (1). Using your cardboard rya guide, cut a few lengths of your selected yarn. Cut them in half again so you have double the amount. Gathering four strands of your wool together, lie them straight and even as if you're going to do a standard rya knot (2).

2. Lie your strands across the pair of warp threads you will be using, and wrap the left-hand side of the strand behind the warp thread (3), above and out through the middle of the warp thread pair (4).

3. With the right-hand side of the strand, do a similar move, wrapping the end behind, above and out through the warp thread pair.

4. Pull the tail of the rya knot down and you'll see it has become an upside down rya knot (5). Continue filling the row with knots.

5. If you are doing multiple rows of the inverted rya, weave a double row of tabby between each row of knots to support them and stop them from twisting loose.

6. Once your field of inverted rya has been filled, fluff them up to standing (6) and give them a trim with the scissors to tidy them up. They can be left long and shaggy, or buzzed right down to a centimetre or so (about half an inch) off the face of the weaving for an almost rug-like texture.

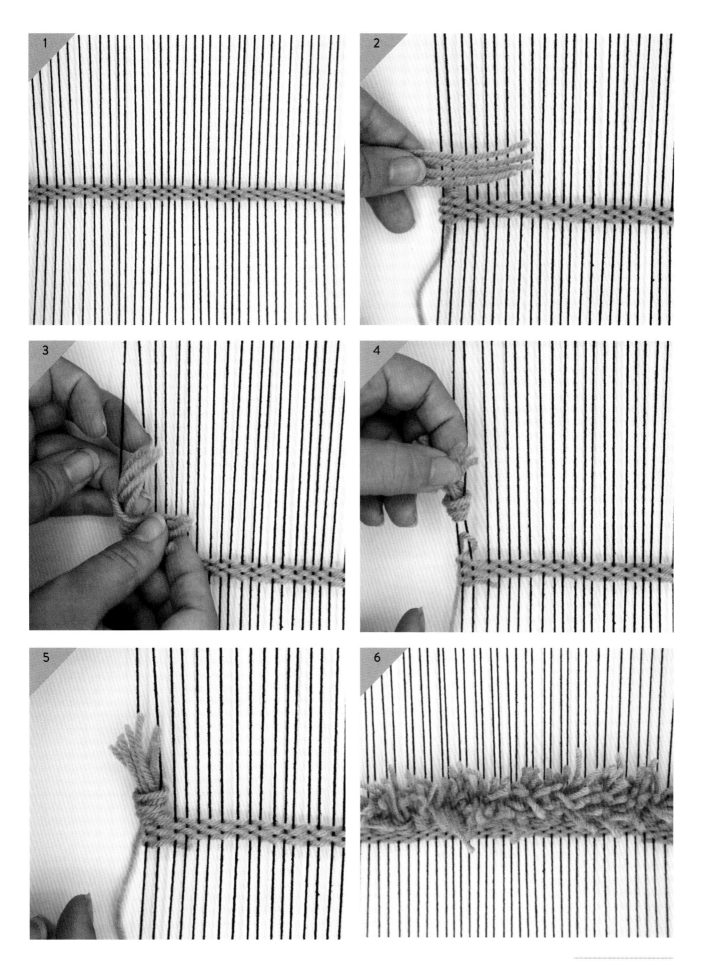

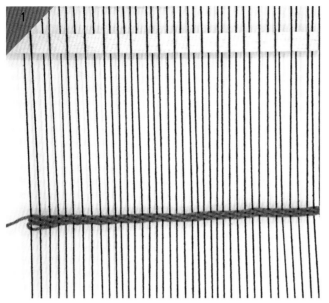
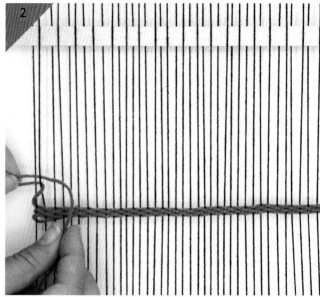

CONTINUOUS RYA

This one is a little different, but pretty easy once you get your head around which direction you're going. It gives great texture for things like hair and is adaptable to fine yarn, multi-strands or chunky yarn. It can spread across the whole width of a loom, or be used in specific patches for texture and interest.

1. Just like all the ryas, you'll need a tabby base (see *Starting a Weave with Tabby*) before you get cracking with this one. As it is a continuous strand technique, you can use a super long length of yarn for one long pass, starting with the tail of the tabby row. Once you've laid down the anchoring rows, you should be back to the left-hand side of the loom with a tail of yarn, ready to start (1).

2. Push a small section of the yarn over the first two warp threads, and back under the second (which should be a tabby 'over'), so a loop is made (2). Taking the loop in your left hand and the yarn tail in your right, fold the loop back over the tail and grab it (3). Pull down with the left hand to pull the yarn through and tighten the knot around the second warp string, and then pull the tail with your right hand until the loop is decreased to your desired length (4). You can tighten the knot again by pulling it down.

3. This should leave the yarn tail exiting to the right of the knot, allowing you to progress across the loom to the right. Repeat the process, pushing the yarn tail under the third warp thread (5), catching the tail with your left hand through the loop, and tightening it to the warp string (6). Complete the process across the loom.

4. When you have completed a full row of continuous rya, weave a double row of tabby over the top to secure it. This should leave you back at the left-hand side of the loom, ready to rya in the opposite direction (7).

5. To move right to left, push a small section of the yarn over the last warp thread and under the second (which should be a tabby 'over'). Taking the loop in your right hand, and holding the tail in your left, grab the tail through the loop. Pull down to tighten the knot around the second warp thread, and pull the tail with your left hand until it is decreased to your desired length.

Very thick yarn may cause over-crowding! If so, knot on every second string, and on the way back in the other direction knot on the string you skipped previously.

Embroidery

There are two main types of embroidery that you will need to know for these pieces. One that is never to be seen, and the other that is to be showcased. The first is a ladder stitch, used to join long vertical panels together to achieve a sharp line in your weave without losing the solid feel, and the other is a back stitch that can add facial features, embellishments and attitude to your weaves.

YOU WILL NEED

> Your completed weave, off the loom, ends tucked in and secured along the bottom

> Standard sewing cotton (for ladder stitch), or three strands of embroidery thread (for back stitch)

> Embroidery or sewing needle

> Scissors

LADDER STITCH

1. For this technique you'll need thread that is similar in colour to the yarn of your weave. Turn your weave over so you are looking at the reverse side. With your cotton doubled up and threaded onto your needle and a substantial knot in the end, slide your needle into one side of a vertical gap, just south of the split (1). I like to anchor it there by doubling back through the doubled thread to make sure it's not going anywhere.

2. Pulling your needle and thread through, shift over to the opposite panel and place your needle in a row or two up, again a few millimetres (⅛in) (2).

3. Continue up the gap, stepping from one side to the other, in a 'Z' formation, threading up the sides every alternating few millimetres (⅛in) until you get to the top of the gap. You can hold the bottom of the ladder and give the thread a gentle pull to ensure it is nice and secure (3), then tie off the end of the thread, and weave it back down the ladder a few millimetres (⅛in) to tie in the end.

BACK STITCH

1. Thread your needle and tie a substantial knot in the end of your embroidery thread. Starting from behind the weave, come up at the starting point of your embroidery (4). Don't pull the thread super taut, as it is easy for the knot to slip through the larger fibres of the yarn. Just secure is just enough.

2. Following your embroidery design, push the needle back down about half a centimetre (¼in) along. Again, if you pull super tight at this point, the thread may disappear into the plush yarn, so gently gently.

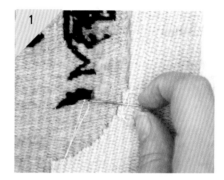

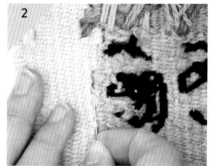

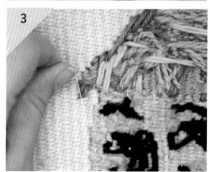

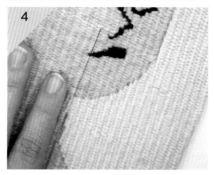

Beading

The final and fun part of decorating your weave is beading. Maybe you want to, maybe you don't. So let's go over a few quick things if *do* you want to.

3. When coming back up to the front, step out another 0.5cm (¼in) along the line (5). Bring the thread up and then, heading backwards, down into the space you went down through last time (6). Continue to the end of the line. Alternatively, bring your needle up in the middle of the previous stitch. This thickens the appearance of the line but maintains a neat shape.

4. This stitch is a good one for curves as well, by shortening the length of the stitch you can get a nice consistent curve. For those keen embroiderers out there, a stem stitch would be a step up from this method for an even more solid line.

If you're wanting to add some embellishments to a mainly tabby weave, look for beads that have a flat side (7). Think coin beads. Sticking a large round bead on a flat surface is gonna be... weird. Unless you're thinking of something like a necklace on a portrait, then a strand of small glass beads would be just the ticket. Have a think about what will work for the piece, and let your creativity go wild.

Secure any bead well, by putting a few stitches through the bead and knotting it to the back of the weave (8), just as you would if you were detailing the hell out of your favourite denim jacket.

If you're adding something like a strand of beads for a necklace, secure the thread the beads will be strung onto by knotting it to a warp thread on the back of the weaving first (9), before bringing the thread to the front of the piece, stringing the beads and securing it the other side with a similar knot (10).

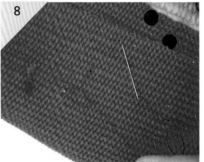

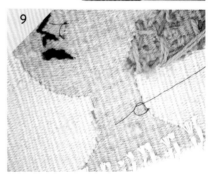

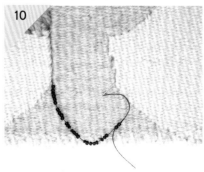

The Projects

Flower Face

This first project is a great one to get you started, because it looks lovely and curvy but it's only as complex as the over under tabby weave, a fringe, and following a template. I've popped in a suggested colour palette so you can follow that, or just go crazy and find some colours of your own! I love to use a flecked/tweed type blend of yarn for the background, because it's just a little more interesting than a flat plain colour but, you know, you do you.

YOU WILL NEED

> Your loom
> Template (see *Templates*)
> Tapestry needle
> Scissors
> Shed stick
> Beater
> Paper spacer, 3cm (1⅛in)
> Measuring tape
> Round dowel for hanger

YARN REQUIRED

> Background and fringe: Light/DK yarn, approx 75g (2¾oz)
> Four flower colours: Light/DK yarn, approx 20g (¾oz) each
> Cotton warp thread, approx 10g (¼oz)

COLOUR PALETTE

1. Before you get your loom all strung up, pop the flower template (see *Templates*) onto the backing and position it so the bottom edge is around 8cm (3¼in) from the bottom of the loom and centred in the frame. Measuring 3cm (1⅛in) from the left side of the bloom, tie your warp string to the bottom nail and start warping (see *Warping Your Loom: Double String Warping*). Go all the way across until you are 3cm (1⅛in) past the right-hand side of the bloom. Once the warp threads are tied off, double check the bloom is in the centre and adjust it until it is. Slide in your paper spacer along the bottom of your loom, and the shed stick in the middle.

2. Take a length of your background yarn about seven times the width of your warp threads, thread it onto your tapestry needle and remembering the bubbling technique (see *Starting a Weave with Tabby*), lay as many rows of tabby up the loom as your base, beating it down against the paper guide to create a straight line. As you finish your last full row, weave the end of the yarn back two warp threads so it is easy to weave into the back later.

3. Referring to the rya making technique (see *Rya Knots*), lay a full row of rya knots above the tabby rows (1). Depending on the type of yarn you're using, you may need anything from four to eight strands of yarn for each knot. Try it out and see how many you need for a full density fringe. If in doubt, go chunkier.

4. Take a length of background yarn and begin weaving in the background between the rya knots and the bottom of the flower on the template, continuing up along the shape to one side, and then adding more yarn to the other side, continuing until the shape begins to curve inwards (see *Using Your Template*).

5. Take your first petal colour and start tabby weaving, filling in the space left by the background yarn, making sure to go from side to side without missing any warp threads, and bubbling the yarn all the way to make sure your tension doesn't get tighter so that the middle starts to pull in like an hourglass. Once you weave all the way up one side, add more yarn to the other side and complete the rest of the first petal shape (2). This should give you the support to weave some more of the background along the right side, as the petal is complete the rest of the first petal shape. Be sure to keep moving the background yarn up each side in line with the template, as the curves of the petals either create support for or require support from the background yarn, depending on the shape of the curve.

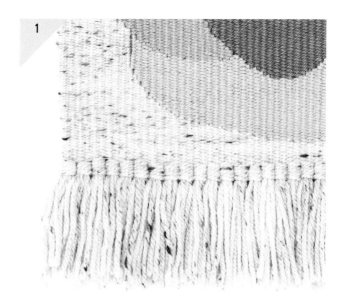

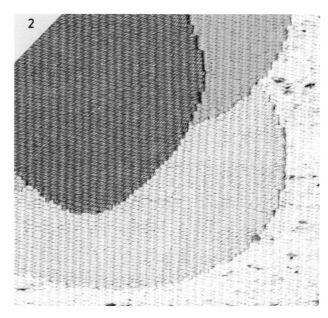

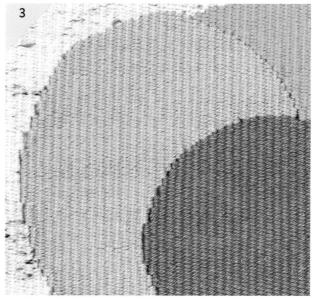

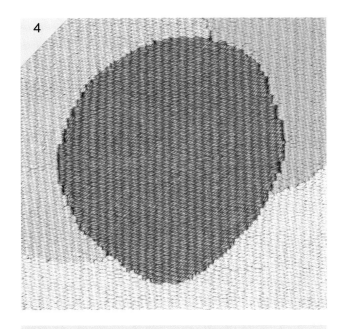

4

If you've got a trail of excess yarn while the shapes are waiting, loop it into a ball and tuck it into the warp strings for safekeeping.

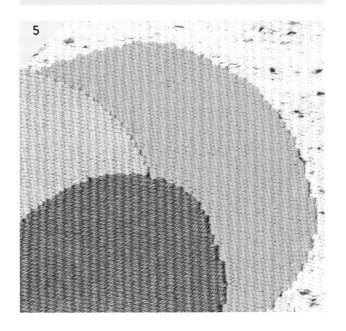

5

6. The next petal you can start weaving is on the far left. You should be able to get almost halfway up it before the centre of the bloom curves in (3). Next let's get going on the flower centre. Grab the yarn you've selected for the centre and, following the template, tabby weave as far up as you can go before the right-hand petal curves out (4). Loop the spare yarn into an out of the way part of your loom (see tip).

7. It's right-hand petal time. You will only weave this petal a couple of dozen rows before the flower centre curves away. Once that happens, take the yarn for the centre again and finish the centre shape (5).

8. Now the centre is complete, the left-hand side petal can be finished, and then finally the right-hand side.

9. Using the background yarn, complete both sides of the background around the bloom, and marry them at the top. Pay attention to the row where the two background sides meet. You don't want two rows stacked on top of each other that going under and over the same warp threads. Each row needs to alternate with the row above and below. If your rows are duplicating at the meeting point, unweave one of the doubled up rows to the side of the weave, cut the yarn leaving a couple of centimetres tail to weave into the back later, and progress with the other yarn, alternating the tabby unders and overs as usual.

10. I am a little particular about the layout of my weavings, so if I have a centred item like this bloom, I like to have the same amount of space on either side of the shape as I do along the top. (The bottom I don't mind about so much because you've got the fringe there doing all its work.) If you're particular too, measure the amount of space on either side of your shape and make sure you weave at least that far past the top of the bloom. If you're not that particular and just want to get the job finished, who am I to stop you?

11. Grab your tape measure and double check the left, centre and right height from the rya knots to the top row of your weaving. If all is straight and true, you can hemstitch your top row, tie in ends and remove your creation from the loom (see *Finishing Your Weaving*). Jump over to *Hanging Your Weaving* to see how to do that, and don't forget to give the ends of the weaving a trim when you've got it hanging up. Hurray! You did it.

Love Those Stems

It's time to get drawing. Grab your sketch pad and design yourself a flower. I've popped in a few inspiration stems in case you get stuck. We're going to try a hand-drawn template and add some bold florally goodness to your home. I've used a chunkier than usual yarn for the front petal to give it some texture that will make people just wanna touch it.

YOU WILL NEED

- A3 sketchpad
- Pencil
- Felt-tip pen
- Your loom
- Tapestry needle
- Scissors
- Shed stick
- Beater
- Paper spacer
- Measuring tape
- Needle and thread
- Beads for embellishment (optional)
- Round dowel for hanger

YARN REQUIRED

- Background and fringe: Light/DK yarn, approx 100g (3½oz)
- Stalk: Light/DK yarn, approx 15g (½oz)
- Leaves: Fine/Baby hand-dyed yarn, approx 15g (½oz)
- Petal 1: Chunky yarn, approx 20g (¾oz)
- Petal 2: Light/DK yarn, approx 15g (½oz)
- Pistil: Chunky yarn, approx 10g (¼oz)
- Cotton warp thread, approx 10g (¼oz)

COLOUR PALETTE

1. Sketch out your flower on your sketch pad, taking up the entire A3 sheet if desired. I like to add a pistil or centre to the flower to add some depth (1). Once you're happy with the design, trace over it in felt-tip pen so it will be easier to see behind the warp strings.

2. Double warp your loom (see *Warping Your Loom: Double String Warping*) to fit the flower and a few centimetres (an inch and a half) of background on either side. Centre the template in the frame and secure the frame backing (see *Using Your Template*).

3. With the paper spacer supporting the bottom of the weave, lay down six rows of tabby in the background yarn (see *Starting a Weave with Tabby*). Using a 10cm (4in) rya cardboard guide, start cutting your lengths for rya knots, for the fringe, from the background colour (see *Rya Knots*), and lay a full row of rya (2).

4. Starting with the background yarn, tabby across the whole loom for as many rows as you need until the stem is introduced (see *Using Your Template*). Then, follow the template up and around the leaves until you get to the top. Weave in the stem and the leaves (3), and then continue working up the template up and around the petals of your flower. Change colours for your petal, and follow the curves on the template using a weft-facing weaving technique (see *Weft-facing Weaving*) if the yarn is a little too chunky for your weaving (4).

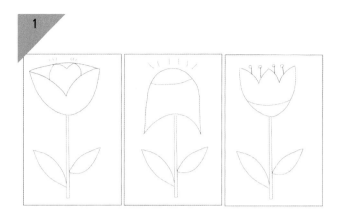

For the leaves, I've used some gorgeous hand-dyed yarn from an independent dyer. Look for small-batch dyers for yarns that create truly amazing effects.

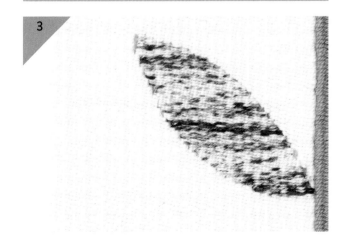

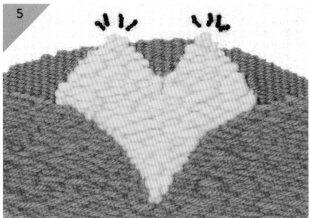

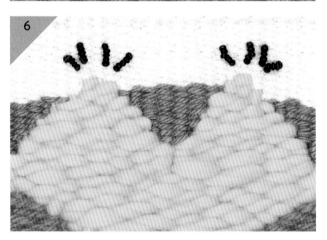

Why not try some chunky wooden beads for a stamen with attitude?

5. For the pistil, thread some chunky yarn onto your needle and use the weft-facing weaving technique to add some dimension and depth to the flower (5). You don't have to be 100% precise when following the shape of the pistil, but create the general curve with your larger yarn.

6. For the top petal, change back to a light/DK yarn and weave the tabby rows to the shape of the chunky yarn. If a row of your chunky yarn takes 2–3 rows of tabby before you get to the next step in, that's fine. You don't want to crush the shape of the pistil by pushing the top petal down too hard on top.

7. Weave as high as you'd like past the top of your flower before checking the top is level, hemstitching and removing the backing from the frame (see *Finishing Your Weaving*). Weave in the ends, making sure to weave them into the same colour areas of your weave.

8. Gently remove your weaving from the loom, lay it on a flat surface and weave the warp bottom thread tails vertically into the tabby below the rya knots. Trim these once woven in so only a millimetre or two (less than ⅛in) stick out (see *Finishing Your Weaving*).

9. Embroidery time! Turn the weaving over so you're working on the reverse, and use your needle and thread to ladder stitch both sides of the stem to the background (see *Embroidery: Ladder Stitch*). You may also want to stitch the vertical sides of the petals to the background to tighten up any gaps there too. Go crazy with a few beads (see *Beading*) (6) and maybe some backstitch lines to decorate the face of your flower with some stamen (see *Embroidery: Back Stitch*).

10. Measure and cut the dowel hanger to size, thread the warp strings onto the hanger, weave each string into the back of the weaving and tie it to its mate (see *Finishing Your Weaving: Hanging Your Weaving*). Weave the ends of the knot into the back of the weave and trim the excess. Lay the weaving flat on a table and gently comb the fringe into shape and trim to the desired length.

Up on High

Step one: Draw some stuff. Step two: Weave it. It's that simple. You're going to design your own abstract weaving for *your* space – your colour palette, your instincts. It's going to be totally original and totally amazing. Because the idea of this piece is bold shapes and soft curves, I'm going to show you a slightly different way to create a template using a drawing app, that will hopefully free up any inhibitions a newbie illustrator may have. Just pick one base colour and three accent colours to act as your palette, and let's get creating.

YOU WILL NEED

> A tablet with a drawing app installed
> A3 sheet of paper
> Pencil
> Your loom
> Tapestry needle
> Scissors
> Shed stick
> Beater
> Measuring tape
> Paper spacer
> Round dowel for hanger

YARN REQUIRED

> Background and fringe: Light/DK yarn, approx 150g (5½oz)
> Colour accents: Light/DK yarn, approx 40g (1½oz) each
> Cotton warp thread, approx 10g (¼oz)

COLOUR PALETTE

1. If you've got a tablet, download a good free drawing app like Adobe Draw. If you're on a computer, find a free drawing website like Kleki. If you're a Luddite, grab your paper and pencil and we'll get to work. Once you've got your drawing surface up and your colour palette chosen, draw up a rectangle shape to work in. If you're using paper, work to the scale of your loom. If you're using tech, any size will do. Pick your first accent colour, adjust your line thickness to the max, and start throwing some curvy line shapes. We're going to incorporate one of the shapes into two parts of the fringe so at the bottom of your drawing, draw a curved line that comes up, through the page and back down. Balance that shape with another similar shape in a different area of the page, slightly curved away or inverted from the first shape. Try and keep the top few centimetres (a couple of inches) of the page clear of shapes so the weaving will be easier to lock off when it's finished (see *Creating a Template*).

2. Using the second accent colour, you want to have some designs running over the edge of each vertical side of the page. Maybe you want some bouncy cloud-type shapes, or maybe some sharp bold shapes.

3. The third accent colour will be for some small shapes that both overlap the existing shapes you've drawn, and also sit on their own on the background. They might be triangle type shapes, blobs, diamonds, whatever you think will work.

4. Once you're happy with your abstract template, if you're on paper, you're ready to go. If you're using tech, turn your screen brightness up and expand your image to size of your template paper, pop the paper over the screen and trace the image directly from the screen onto your paper, shuffling it around until you've copied the entire image. Now, we weave.

5. Pop your template in the centre of your frame (1), and attach it to the back board 5cm (2in) above the bottom of your loom to leave room for the paper spacer, tabby and rya rows. Double string your loom to the size of your template (see *Warping Your Loom: Double String Warping*), so the edges of the vertical shapes align with the outermost warp strings. Using the background yarn, pull a length of yarn that is about seven times the width of your warp strings and lay down around six rows of tabby (see *Starting a Weave with Tabby*).

I like to use thick embroidery thread to stitch some random line patterns, and also add on some flat-faced wooden beads for a high-impact look.

6. With the 10cm (4in) rya cardboard guide in your hot little hands, wrap your background yarn around it and cut the yarn through the middle for your rya knots (see *Rya Knots*). Start laying your row of rya knots until you hit the section where your accent colour line comes through the bottom of your page. Cut a number of rya knot lengths using the first accent colour and pop in some knots in the new colour to show where the line passes through on your template. Continue cutting and laying the remainder of the rya knots in the background colour until the other end of the accent line on the template cuts through. Lay knots in the accent colour, swapping back to the background colour if your template requires it (2).

7. Having all your yarns on hand, start weaving up the frame, following the template where the accent colours take over from the background, where accent one overlaps with accent two and three, and work your way all the way up your design (see *Using Your Template*).

8. Make sure you've left about 3cm (1⅛in) of plain background weave at the top, then measure to ensure the weave is even, before locking it off with hemstitch (see *Finishing Your Weaving*). Weave in all your ends, cut and knot the warp strings and remove the weave from the loom.

9. Now you can hang your weave as it is, or you can have a little bit of fun and add some embroidery embellishments (3) or even some beading to add another dimension onto your weave (see *Embroidery: Back Stitch* and *Beading*).

10. Measure the width of the top of your weaving, add 6cm (2⅜in) and cut your dowel rod to size. See *Finishing Your Weaving: Hanging Your Weaving* to attach the weaving to the rod, and enjoy!

A Pair

For this project, we're going to step away from sexy curved lines and smooth details and instead use some techniques to add volume, boldness and a little punch to your work. The goal won't be to hide the warp threads in this one, but to embrace the structure of the weaving process. We're also embellishing the fringe here with a double tier of rya knots, because why not?

YOU WILL NEED

> Your loom
> Template (see *Templates*)
> Tapestry needle
> Scissors
> Shed stick
> Beater
> Paper spacer
> Measuring tape
> Round dowel for hanger

YARN REQUIRED

> Base fringe: Super chunky yarn, approx 30g (1oz)
> Background and fringe: Chunky yarn, approx 60g (2¼oz)
> Two leaf colours: Light yarn, approx 15g (½oz) each
> Four flower accent colours: Chunky to super chunky yarn, approx 10g (¼oz) each
> Stalk: Light to medium yarn, approx 2m (2¼yd)
> Cotton warp thread, approx 10g (¼oz)

COLOUR PALETTE

Design Diaries: Creative Process in Graphic Design

1. Copy the template (see *Templates*) and centre it on your loom backing board. Single string your loom so the flowers have some background space on either side (see *Warping Your Loom: Single String Warping*). I warped mine up to 37cm (14½in) wide.

2. Take a length of your background yarn that is six widths of the warp strings, and lay a series of tabby rows (see *Starting a Weave with Tabby*). If you're going without the spacer (see tip) measure your six starter tabby rows from the bottom of your loom to make sure they're straight before you start on the rya.

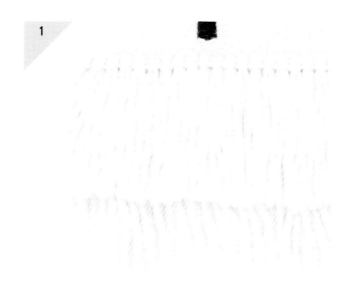

If you feel most comfortable using the paper spacer to support the bottom row of your weaving, carry on using one. If you think you've got a handle on pressure when you're compressing your rows, try it without.

3. Using the 10cm (4in) rya guide, wind the super chunky yarn around enough times so you have one strand for each pair of warp strings. Use the rya knot technique (see *Rya Knots*) to lay a row of single threads of the super chunky. Next, lay another six anchor rows of tabby above the super chunky, using your background yarn, and lay second a row of rya knots for a full density fringe on top using the same (1).

4. Using the background yarn, start weaving to the template (see *Using Your Template*). For the leaves, use the inverted rya technique to fill the leaf area with little bundles of rya knots (see *Inverted and Continuous Rya: Inverted Rya*) (2), securing each rya row with three tabby rows. Continue this process as you move up the shape of the leaf (3).

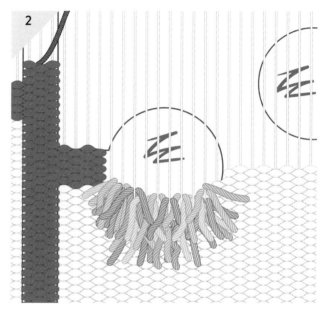

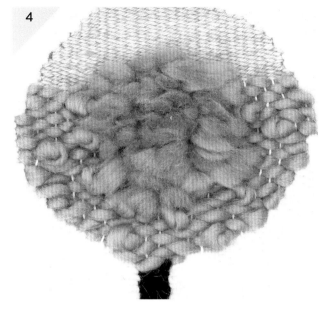

5. For the stems, tabby across the warp threads, which should be about two strings wide. Watch your tension here as it's easy to pull those two rows closer together as you work your way up. Start weaving in the background colour, working your way around the flowerhead shapes. Use the weft-facing weaving technique (see *Weft-facing Weaving*) for the chunky petals of the flowers (4). Watch out for any accidental patterns forming like over 3 under 1 over 3 under 1, and keep changing with two jumps and four jumps so it looks nice and random.

6. I chose the continuous rya technique (see *Inverted and Continuous Rya: Continuous Rya*) for the centre of one flower, and for the other I used the chunkiest yarn to wrap 4cm (1½in) lengths around every second warp thread, anchoring each row with some tabby (5). Next pick up your background colour and weave it to the top (6). I took mine 4cm (1½in) above the flowers.

7. Measure the weave to check the top row is straight, then finish it off (see *Finishing Your Weaving*). While you've got those scissors to hand, give the leaves a buzz cut. Give the fibres in the leaves a little ruffle and brush them upright if some have been crushed. Holding the scissors horizontal to the weaving, carefully trim the yarn to an even height. I like some dimension so I trim some off the sides to give a nice soft edge.

8. Remove your weave from the loom (see *Finishing Your Weave: Cutting It Off the Loom*). Have a look how the piece is holding together. If the stalks or the sides of the flowers are gaping, you may want to pop in a row of ladder stitch to lock it all together (see *Embroidery: Ladder Stitch*). Finally, see *Finishing Your Weaving: Hanging Your Weaving* for how to hang the piece.

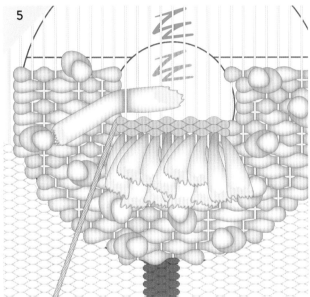

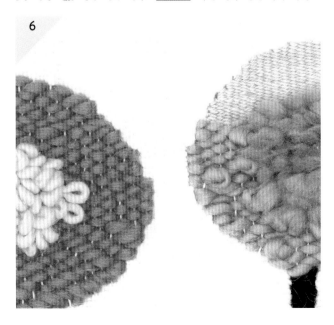

Bright Dorky Love

Get ready – you're going to be making your own typography piece. With this project, we're going to learn how to put all those geometry lessons in high school to good use, to create a simple template with four even boxes surrounded by equal background space, and then we're going to gently nestle your typography in each box. The result will be a lovely, square, equal, pleasing typography image that's hopefully not going to make any graphic designer friends who may see it want to claw their eyes out. Have fun with your colour selection and let's get templating.

YOU WILL NEED

> Your loom
> A couple of sheets of plain paper
> Tape
> Pencil and eraser
> Felt-tip pen
> Drawing compass
> Ruler
> Tapestry needle
> Sewing needle and thread
> Scissors
> Shed stick
> Beater
> Paper spacer
> Measuring tape
> Round dowel for hanger

YARN REQUIRED

> Background and fringe: Medium/worsted yarn, approx 75g (2¾oz)
> Six bright colours: Light/DK yarn, approx 20g (¾oz) each
> Cotton warp thread, approx 10g (¼oz)

COLOUR PALETTE

1. To create your template, measure the width of your loom, across the face when warped. Using that measurement, measure, cut and tape together a square template from your paper. Measure 3cm (1⅛in) in from each side of the paper and draw in the border. From this inner square, measure and mark the centre lines both vertically and horizontally. Do you have four equal squares? Perfect. Now measure and mark a line 1.5cm (⅝in) out from either side of those vertical and horizontal lines. Still four equal squares? Brilliant. These are the boxes your lettering will go in.

2. Starting with the L, draw in a vertical rectangle 4cm (1½in) wide, touching the left side of the square and the top and bottom. Measure out the horizontal rectangle along the bottom, again 4cm (1½in) high.

3. E time. Draw in another 4cm (1½in) wide rectangle on the left side, and three equal 4cm (1½in) rectangles to complete the letter.

4. Now the V. Mark the middle of the bottom line of the square. Nestle your 4cm (1½in) wide rectangles into the middle of the top corners, with the bottom edge meeting at the centre point of the bottom line.

5. Let's round out the LOVE with the O. Use your compass to draw in a circle that will hit all sides of the box. After the larger O has been drawn, wind in the compass by 4cm (1½in) and draw in the inner circle.

6. Trace back over your shapes with a felt-tip pen, and decide where you want to break them up for the colour blocking. I broke my L so the bottom edge is the long edge, as I wanted the E to have a long vertical. I sliced my O on the diagonal but you might want a cleaner look of a slice across the middle or down the centre. Plot out what colour will go where, making sure to get a good mix of warm and cool colours on all sides of your design. Step back from your template, have a look from a distance and see if anything stands out that you want to change before it is committed to the loom.

7. Once your template is complete (1), secure it to the backing of your loom, leaving at least 7cm (2¾in) from the bottom of your loom to where the template starts. Remember, the entire piece of paper is the template, not just the pencilled in 3cm (1⅛in) border. Warp your loom with single strings (see *Warping Your Loom: Single String Warping*), and check your template is centred.

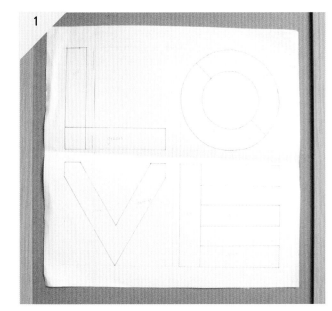

You can have a little fun with this piece as far as yarn choice goes. As long as each yarn is a similar weight, you can use a combination of fibres here. I used some pure wool, some acrylics and some cotton yarns.

You may want each rainbow rya knot to be the same colour, you may want to limit the colour mix. As long as your knots are the same thickness, do what feels right.

3

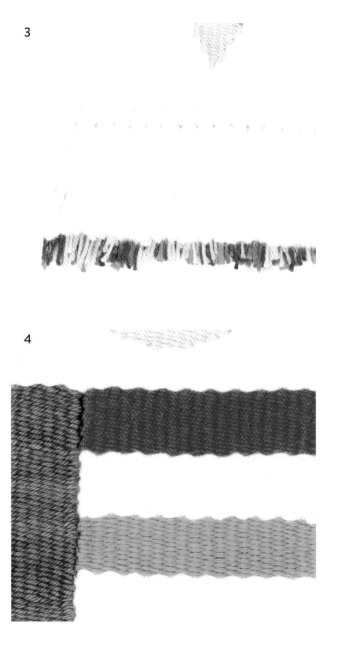

4

8. Weave in around four to six supporting tabby rows using the background yarn (see *Starting a Weave with Tabby*), leaving a gap of at least 3cm (1⅛in) between the bottom of the loom and your weaving. Go grab that lovely rainbow selection of yarns, and using the 10cm (4in) rya guide, cut a bunch of strands of each colour (2). To create the confetti rainbow fringe, you're going to mix these up into countless colour combinations. Work your way across the row, laying a full row of rya knots using a mixture of these colours (see *Rya Knots*).

9. Next, lay an additional six rows of tabby in your background colour across the top of the confetti rainbow fringe. Then use the 10cm (4in) rya guide to cut a full density fringe using the background colour and knot it over the top (3). Adjust your template so the bottom edge of your paper is sitting right behind the top rya row, and start weaving up that template (see *Using Your Template*), along and around the lettering, weaving in your rainbow blocks for the letter shapes and watching that the sides aren't creeping in and messing up the square shape we're aiming for (4).

10. Once you've finished weaving the template design, check everything is even and follow the instructions in *Finishing Your Weaving* to tidy up and remove your weave from the loom.

11. Using your needle and thread, stitch up the vertical gaps around the letters, making for a tight fit together with the background yarn (see *Embroidery: Ladder Stitch*). Measure the width of the top of your weaving and cut your round dowel to the width plus 6cm (2⅜in) before attaching it to the rod (see *Finishing Your Weaving: Hanging Your Weaving*).

12. Once the piece is hanging, gently comb both layers of fringe into place and starting with the rainbow confetti fringe, give it a gentle trim for a straight edge. Depending on how much of the rainbow fringe you'd like on display, do the same for the fringe woven with the background yarn, trimming it into a straight line either just skimming the rainbow feature, or a few centimetres (an inch or so) up to really show it off.

Blush Breeze

Now you're going to learn how to mix fine yarns together to create a new colour pattern, and make a gradient of colours slide up the loom. I've chosen colours that are of a similar shade to make a dark to light fade. Once you've got a handle on the technique, you can aim to fade very different colours into each other through a gradient spectrum.

YOU WILL NEED

> Your loom
> Tapestry needle
> Scissors
> Shed stick
> Beater
> Measuring tape
> Paper and pencil for template
> Round dowel for hanger

YARN REQUIRED

> Background and top fringe: Medium/worsted yarn, approx 60g (2¼oz)
> Accent fringe trim: Double the width of your piece, plus a little extra
> Contrast colour: Light/worsted yarn, approx 20g (¾oz)
> Cotton warp thread, approx 10g (¼oz)

COLOUR PALETTE

FIELD	DARK	MEDIUM	LIGHT
G			III
F		I	II
E		II	I
D		III	
C	I	II	
B	II	I	
A	III		

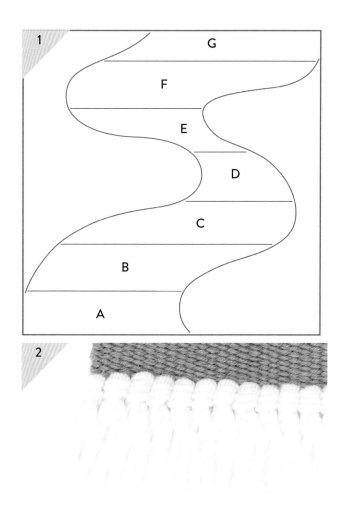

1. Draw up a template to fit within the width and height of your loom (see *Creating a Template*), featuring a curvy flowing shape down the middle. The goal is to have three strands of fine yarn for each row of the gradient feature, so plot up a little plan as shown (1), separating your gradient flow into seven equal sections, and marking up which section will have which combination of colours, as shown in the table.

2. Once it is planned and plotted, affix the template to your loom and single warp the loom over the top of it, making sure the template is centred (see *Warping Your Loom: Singe String Warping*). Begin by laying six rows of tabby (see *Starting a Weave with Tabby*) and then a full density row of rya knots (see *Rya Knots*) in the background colour (2).

3. Cut three long strands of the darkest colour. Thread all three onto your tapestry needle, and using the template as the guide, start weaving the curvy shape (see *Using Your Template*). As you pull your yarn through the warp threads, give it a gentle twist, so each row is a twist of all three yarns and not the three threads stacked on top of each other (3). Continue weaving the A section until you are at the line on the template that shows where the next section starts.

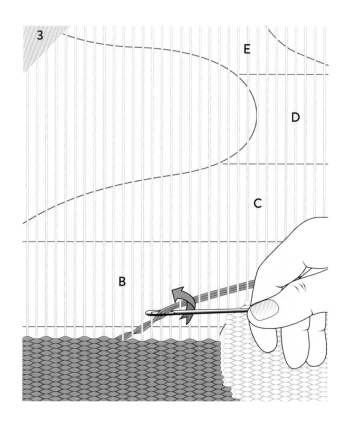

Step back from your weaving every so often while you're blending to check that no sneaky clumps of colour have formed while you weren't watching.

4. Once you hit the B section, weave a row of the A combination of yarns, but skipping two 'overs' in the row. Space these skips out so they are not next to each other but about one third and two thirds across the shape (4). Pull out a new combination of yarn: two lengths dark and one length of the medium colour. Thread that onto a tapestry needle and weave the latest row, only weaving 'over' the two skipped sections. The next row, weave another full row of the A combination, and then a row with three random skips of the overs, coming back and weaving them in with the B combination again. In the next row, A will be the dominant colour again, but with four skips for the B combination to fill in. Once you've reached a stage where the B combination is weaving in almost half of the row, that will become the dominant one, with the A combination phasing out by filling in four, then three, then two skips, before it is finished.

5. Once you've phased out the A combination, continue twisting the yarns together as you tabby weave the B section, and repeat the process as you approach the C section, introducing a thread with two medium and one dark coloured yarn.

6. As you work your way along the gradient, make sure you're also weaving up the background on either side to help the curve take shape as it moves up the loom (5).

7. Once you've made it through all the transitions from one section to the next and you're at the top of the template, measure to check your weave is nice and even, and pop a hemstitch along the top using the background colour (see *Finishing Your Weaving*).

8. Finally, pop the back out of your loom to weave in and trim up the ends, cut the piece off the loom and follow the instructions in *Finishing Your Weaving: Hanging Your Weaving* to do what you need to do to hang that baby up!

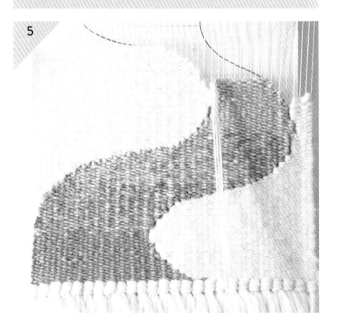

Get in Line

It's time to break out your primary (elementary) school maths skills, because we're gonna crunch the numbers to create a geometrical beauty for your wall. This project is based around a 12 square design, but you can tweak the pattern to fit your loom. Let your imagination go for a wander and come back with a fun palette that's going to suit your home. I've used four key colours, plus black and white to contrast, but the combinations are endless and totally up to you.

YOU WILL NEED

> Your loom
> Tapestry needle
> Scissors
> Shed stick
> Beater
> Measuring tape
> Two sheets of A3 paper
> Sticky tape
> Coloured pencils/markers to match your yarn
> Sewing cotton and needle
> Maths brain/calculator
> Round dowel for hanger

YARN REQUIRED

> Fringe: Light/DK yarn, approx 40g (1½oz)
> Neutral background: Light/DK yarn, approx 50g (1¾oz)
> Four pattern colours: Light/DK yarn, approx 40g each (1½oz)
> Cotton warp thread, approx 10g (¼oz)

COLOUR PALETTE

1. First we have to calculate how many squares your loom can handle, and what size they will be. The length of your frame is the most important measurement to start with. Measure from the top nails to the bottom ones. Mine is 61cm (24in). You'll need a spare 12cm (4¾in) to make room for a 4cm (1½in) gap at the bottom to tie warp strings off, 2cm (¾in) for base tabby and rya knots, 2cm (¾in) for the top row and locking stitch and 4cm (1½in) for warp strings to hang the piece from. That is 49cm (19¼in) on my loom. 49 ÷ 4 = 12.25. Round that down to 12cm (4¾in) and there is the dimension of your squares. It's always easier to work with round numbers and have a little wiggle room. Next, just double check that your loom is wide enough to fit three squares across at that size. My loom is 38cm (15in) across, so 12 x 3 = 36cm (14½in). Perfect. That's the size we will string the loom to.

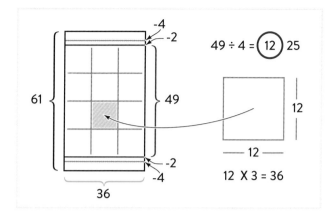

2. Now we template. Tape the long edge of the A3 sheets together and cut it to the total size of your four-by-three-squares shape, with a 1cm (½in) border around it. Measure out and pencil draw your four-by-three-squares grid, the side of each square will be 12cm (4¾in). Take time to ensure your lines are straight because it will break hearts later if your template line starts to veer away from your straight warp threads. Once you have your grid, start patterning. I've drawn in a few patterns you can use (1). Step back every so often to get the overall look and feel. You might see patterns in the randomness that you want to break up.

3. Next, start plotting the colours of your pattern. I've chosen a mix of four colours plus a neutral background, but you might choose two hero colours and a background colour, or go bananas with nine or ten different shades. Who am I to judge? Colour in the template so you have a guide while you're weaving.

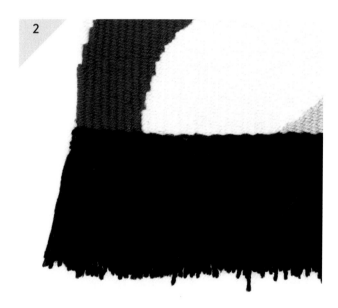

4. Template done, pop it onto your loom, centred vertically and horizontally in the frame, with the template design starting 6cm (2⅜in) from the bottom of your loom. Check the width of the three squares (mine is 36cm/14¼in) and double warp your loom

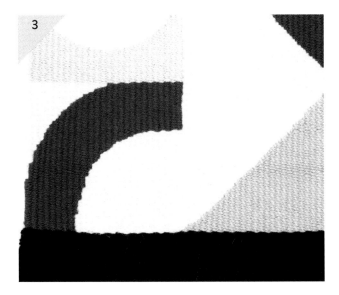

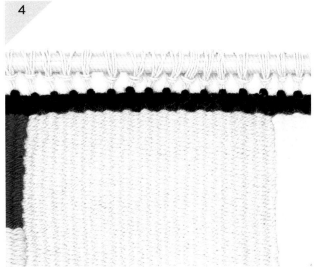

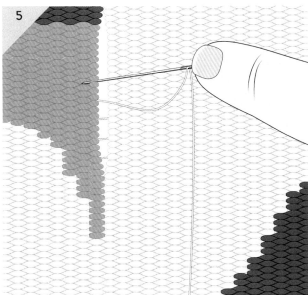

to that size (see *Warping Your Loom: Double String Warping*). Lay your tabby (see *Starting a Weave with Tabby*) and rya knots (see *Rya Knots*), and pop an additional four rows of tabby above that in the fringe colour, so the squares all have a strong straight base to start from (2). Adjust your template vertically up or down so it is starting where those last tabby rows finish.

5. Following your template (see *Using Your Template*), start working up the loom along all the lines, angles and edges of your patterns (3). Where the coloured edge of one square matches the corresponding edge of its neighbour, feel free to weave across the vertical gap of the square row to merge the vertical panels together.

6. Once you are at the top and all the panels are finished and at the same height, lay 1–2cm (½–¾in) of tabby in the fringe contrast colour along the top to bring all the panels together again (4). Hemstitch along the top, and tidy the dark side of the loom, before removing the weave (see *Finishing Your Weaving*).

7. Starting at one end, secure a doubled-up length of sewing cotton at the top of one vertical panel, and ladder stitch your way to the bottom of the panel (see *Embroidery: Ladder Stitch*) (5). Continue until ladder stitches bind all vertical gaps between the squares and the weaving is one solid piece.

8. My warp strings weren't long enough for the traditional way of hanging the weaving, so I double looped each string around the rod. This leaves a bit of negative space between the weaving and the rod, for something different for this technique see *Finishing Your Weave: Hanging Your Weaving, moderate option.*

9. Finally, lay the weaving flat on a table, gently comb the fringe into shape, and trim any shaggy ends into a nice straight line.

Girl's Got Hair

We are about to step into some cartoon people weaving action so grab your template – we're gonna have some fun! With this project, you've got a choice of hair-dos for this lovely lady. Change up the colours, give her a purple sweater and teal hair, or maybe a white background will suit your home better. Go for it!

YOU WILL NEED

> Your loom
> Template (see *Templates*)
> Marker pen
> Tapestry needle
> Embroidery needle
> Black cotton thread
> Scissors
> Shed stick
> Beater
> Paper spacer
> Measuring tape
> Round dowel for hanger

YARN REQUIRED

> Background and fringe: Light/DK yarn, approx 100g (3½oz)
> Sweater and fringe: Light/DK yarn, approx 15g (½oz)
> Hair: Light/DK yarn, approx 30g (1oz)
> Skin: Fine/Baby yarn, approx 15g (½oz)
> Lips: Light/DK yarn, approx 20cm (8in) length
> Cotton warp thread, approx 10g (¼oz)

COLOUR PALETTE

1. Trace the hair design you intend to weave onto the template with a marker pen so it is easier to follow. Centre the template on your loom and nestle it 6cm (2⅜in) from the bottom edge. Double warp your loom to approx 33cm (13in) wide (see *Warping Your Loom: Double String Warping*), or wide enough that the template image is centred on your loom with some background space surrounding her hair.

2. With a paper spacer guide supporting the space between the bottom of the frame and 6cm (2⅜in) below the start of the sweater on the template, lay six rows of tabby in the background yarn (see *Starting a Weave with Tabby*).

3. Using a 10cm (4in) rya cardboard guide, start cutting your lengths for rya knots from the background colour (see *Rya Knots*). My yarn required eight strands per knot but you should adjust that depending on your yarn, and you will need approximately 23 rya knots. Start weaving them in from the left of the loom, and continue along the line until you hit the sweater on the template. Work your way in from the right-hand side using the background colour, again until you reach the sweater.

4. Using the 10cm (4in) rya guide, get your sweater yarn and begin to measure and cut yarn for some more rya knots. Again, six to eight strands per knot depending on the yarn, and you will need approx 11 rya knots. Thread those into the loom where the sweater is indicated, filling up the rest of the row (1).

Part of what I love so much about weaving is that it is an amalgamation of so many mediums, so if you're a doodler, a sketcher or a painter of people, weaving your work is such a fun way to flex your creative muscle. And who doesn't love to draw a gorgeous lady and give her some to-die-for hair?

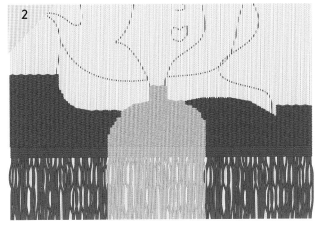

5. Threading a length of sweater yarn onto your tapestry needle, start tabby weaving the sweater, following along the template as the shoulders taper and the neck rises. Next, start weaving the background to the left and the right, tabby weaving between the edge and the sweater, and around the template when the hair begins. As the hair moves and the background takes an inside curve, start working the hair and then the face and lips up and up, weaving the dominant colour of the shape until the next needs to take over (2). Continue following the template to the top of the hair.

6. Weave at least 2cm (¾in) past the top of the hair, or as high as you'd like, before checking the top is level, hemstitching across, removing the backing from the frame and weaving in the ends (see *Finishing Your Weaving*). Remove your weave from the loom.

7. Embroidery time! Because there are a fair few vertical gaps around the sweater, the neck and the face, I like to ladder stitch these areas together so the weave is nice and tight and the gaps are not as obvious (see *Embroidery: Ladder stitch*). Using the template as your guide, back stitch the nose, eyes and brows into place (see *Embroidery: Back stitch*) (3).

8. Cut your dowel hanger to size, then thread the warp strings onto the hanger, weave each string into the back of the weaving, and tie it to its mate. Weave the ends of the knot into the back of the weave and trim the excess (see *Finishing Your Weaving*). Finally, lie the weaving flat on a table and gently comb the fringe into shape, trimming any shaggies off the end to get a nice straight line.

Why not add a fabulous beaded necklace to complete her look?

Mo Bro

Now you've had a go at a cartoon portrait, let's step it up a little and add some volume, texture and chunky yarns, as well as a bit of your own style. The template (see *Templates*) provides some options for your old bloke: adjusting his hairstyle, mo style and shirt style. Roving will help you achieve the fluffiest and most luxurious moustache, but if that's not your thing, using the inverted rya technique with a more standard yarn will have a similar effect.

YOU WILL NEED

> Your loom
> Template (see *Templates*)
> Tapestry needle
> Large sewing scissors
> Shed stick
> Beater
> Measuring tape
> Black sewing cotton
> Sewing needle
> Round dowel for hanger

YARN REQUIRED

> Background and fringe: Light yarn, approx 60g (2¼oz)
> Shirt: Super chunky yarn, approx 25g (1oz)
> Skin: Chunky yarn, approx 20g (¾oz)
> Moustache: Roving, approx 30g (1oz) and a scrap of chunky yarn in the same colour
> Hair: Chunky yarn, approx 15g (½oz)
> Cotton warp thread, approx 5g (⅛oz)

COLOUR PALETTE

1. Using the template (see *Templates*), choose and mark up the outlines for hair, moustache and shirt. Seeing as we're using chunky yarn and there aren't too many line details, single string your loom to the width you want your piece (see *Warping Your Loom: Single String Warping*). Secure the template behind the warp strings, and thread in your paper guide at the bottom of the loom and the shed stick through the middle.

2. Using your background colour, lay six rows of tabby across the bottom (see *Starting a Weave with Tabby*), and then a full row of rya knots (see *Rya Knots*). Adjust the template so the image starts at the rya knots, and start weaving in the chest of the shirt using a weft-facing weaving technique (see *Weft-facing Weaving*) that leaves enough space between the weft so that it is not congested and pushing the strings out of shape (1). Continue up the template (see *Using Your Template*) switching to a tabby weave for the background colour in the space between the chest and the arms, and the weft-facing weaving for the sleeves again. Tabby weave the face colour, right up until you hit the moustache, and catch the background colour up to the same point so you have an even line of weaving before starting on the moustache.

3. To start on your moustache, add two or three rows of tabby as a base, using chunky yarn in the same colour as the roving. Take your length of roving and trim the end to a blunt end. Cut an 8cm (3¼in) length of roving to start with, and pinch off a small section of fibre, a similar thickness to the chunky yarn you used in the sweater. Thread that around one of the warp threads of the moustache area. Keep pinching off similar sized sections of the roving and threading them around alternating warp threads for one whole row of the moustache (2). Once you have laid a full row of moustache fluff, take a similar shade yarn (generally the hair colour), and lay three rows of tabby over the top of it to secure the row but not crush it down. Repeat the process layering roving into the moustache area and securing it with a few rows of tabby until the moustache is completely filled in, ending the shape on the roving, not the tabby (3).

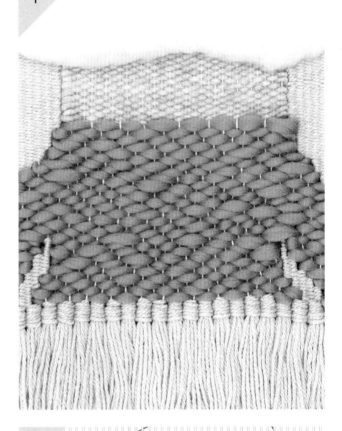

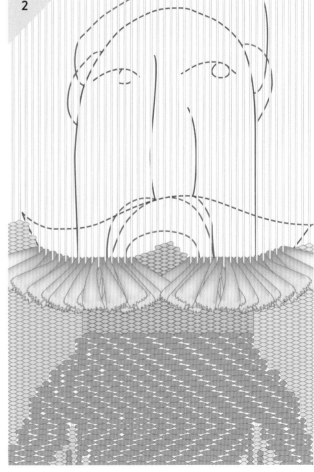

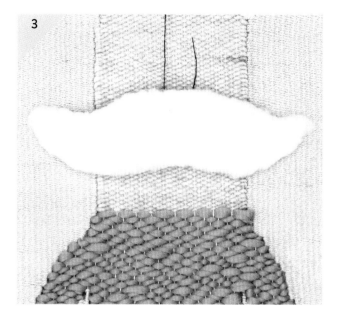

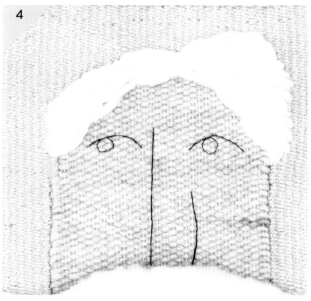

4. Continue following the template, tabby weaving the background and the face up the loom, and working in the tabby weave for the hair when the template indicates. Continue up the background at least 3cm (1⅛in) past the shape of the head. Measure to ensure the weaving is straight, lock it off with hemstitch, and tidy the reverse (see *Finishing Your Weaving*).

5. Next use the chunky hair yarn, and start over-weaving the hair sections in the direction of the natural hair flow (see *Overweaving*), until all the tabby is covered with strands of hair (4).

6. It's time to trim that moustache. I find it easier if it is still on the loom and under tension. First, fluff up the roving so it is all standing straight up – we want everything at its most voluminous before the cut. Lay your loom down on a table and looking at it from the side, make a cut as flat as you can, right across the top, so it is about the height of your first knuckle all the way across. Once the moustache is level across the top, you can start trimming it into shape around the corners, taking the high sides off all the edges, cutting into the joins and rounding the sides to gently fade into the flat top.

7. Once your moustache is on point, cut and tie off the warp threads and remove the piece from your loom (see *Finishing Your Weaving: Cutting It Off the Loom*).

8. Now the old fella needs a face. Using your needle and some black thread, embroider a great honking nose and some eyes on that mug using a simple back stitch (see *Embroidery: Back Stitch*).

9. Follow the instructions in *Finishing Your Weaving: Hanging Your Weaving* to add the hanging dowel and finish off the piece. There he is! Will he have a name?

Trimming the moustache is easier if you use a large pair of sewing scissors so you can easily match the depth of each cut, but if you only have embroidery scissors, just take it slow and you'll be fine.

Peace, Sister

Oooh! One of my favourite looks. This CMYK overlay effect is one that takes a bit of focus at the template level, but once the design is sorted it's no harder to weave than anything else and it serves up such a punchy, graphic, modern look. Don't think that you are restricted to cyan, magenta, yellow and black. You could use the overlay effect with shades of one colour like grey or pink, starting lighter from the outside and increasing the colour strength until you get to the centre.

YOU WILL NEED

> Your loom
> Peace sign template (see *Templates*) or your own similar sized icon
> A3 paper for template
> Pencil
> Felt-tip pen
> Tapestry needle
> Scissors
> Shed stick
> Beater
> Measuring tape
> Round dowel for hanger

YARN REQUIRED

> Background and fringe: 8 ply, approx 75g (2¾oz)
> Six to seven colours for the overlay: approx 20g (¾oz) each
> Cotton warp thread, approx 10g (¼oz)

COLOUR PALETTE

1. Cut out the template (see *Templates*), place it centrally on a blank piece of A3 paper, and trace around the shape in pencil. Pivot the template so it is half on and half off the centre image. You can play around with shifting it up and down also. Trace around it again. Now shift the template to the right and again, play around with the overlap, bearing in mind that the centre will be where the colours intersect. Trace around the shape before going over all your lines with felt-tip pen so they stand out behind the warp strings.

2. Working from the outside in, start with the parts of each image that aren't overlapping with anything. Mark each one as either Y for yellow, M for magenta or C for cyan. Now find the areas where two of those primary colours are overlappingg and label those as the secondary colours of red, green or blue. Where all secondary colours overlap each other, you've got your black section (1). If you're a visual person, you may want to colour in each section with marker pens or coloured pencils.

3. Attach your completed template to the backing of your loom and get warping (see *Warping Your Loom: Double String Warping*). It's helpful to decide how much background you want around each side of the image, and warp the loom to fit that measurement.

4. Lay your tabby in the background colour (see *Starting a Weave with Tabby*), then your rya knots (see *Rya Knots*) and start tabby weaving the background (2) in until you need to split it apart to follow the template (see *Using Your Template*). Pay special attention to the picture overall, because it is easy to miss a change in the template and suddenly your overlap section is running away with itself.

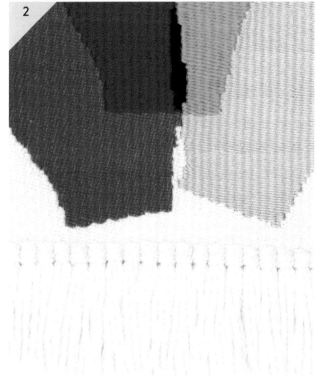

3

Depending on where your loyalties lie within the acrylic vs natural fibre convo, this is a great project to go for the bright, vibrant acrylics to get a slew of colour options.

5. Continue up the template until you're past the image and back into the background (3). Leaving the same amount of space above as below it so the image is centred. Measure to make sure the weaving is straight, add an additional three to four rows of tabby and lock off the top (see *Finishing Your Weaving*).

6. See *Finishing Your Weaving* for instructions on tidying up the reverse and removing the weave from your loom. For this particular design, I had some vertical gaps in the weave from the straight lines of the fingers (4), so I tightened them up with a few ladder stitches (see *Embroidery: Ladder Stitch*).

7. Hang your weaving according to the instruction in *Finishing Your Weaving: Hanging Your Weaving*, and don't forget to give the loose ends a trim when you've got it hanging up.

4

Summer Recall

Now for something a little different, because that loom of yours is versatile, baby. We're going to work on the whole loom but produce four individual pieces. No one said your whole loom has to be strung all the way across, so here we go on a themed grouping. I've chosen some lovely little sweet treats and included a template, but if you want to try out a set of little woodland creatures, or blooms or whatever your heart desires, let's do it.

YOU WILL NEED

> Your loom
> Template (see *Templates*) or at least two pieces of plain A4 paper
> Tapestry needle
> Scissors
> Shed stick
> Beater
> Measuring tape
> Sewing needle and thread
> Four round dowels for hangers

YARN REQUIRED

> Background and fringe: Light yarn, approx 75g (2¾oz)
> Ice block accents: Light yarn, approx 10g (¼oz) each
> Cotton warp thread, approx 10g (¼oz)

COLOUR PALETTE

1. First work out the size and how many weaves your loom can handle. My loom surface is 60cm (23½in) high by 38cm (15in) wide. You'll need at least 5cm (2in) of space at the top and the bottom, and a 12cm (4¾in) gap in the middle. Divide the remaining space by two and you have the height of your weavings. Mine was 19cm (7½in). It's up to you how wide you make the pieces, but I like to leave a comfortable space between the separate weavings, so mine will be 15cm (6in) wide.

2. Using the dimensions for your four individual weavings, draw up some templates for your pieces (see *Creating a Template*) if you're not using the ones I've provided (see *Templates*). Knowing the full height including the placement of the first tabby line will help you see where to start and stop each piece, so make sure your template reflects the full size of what you'll be working on. Put the backing into your loom, then noting the space required at the bottom and middle of the loom, stick your templates into position and double string the loom (see *Warping Your Loom: Double String Warping*), tying off the left side at the 15cm (6in) point, and leaving a gap before double stringing the right to a width of 15cm (6in). Remember your paper guide along the bottom if your tabby lines are still a little wobbly. The height is key here so better to be safe than sorry.

3. Starting with the background colour, lay six rows of tabby for each of the bottom two weaves (see *Starting a Weave with Tabby*). As these are mini weaves, we'll halve the size of the rya knots also. Using the 10cm (4in) rya guide, wind the background yarn around the card several times and cut the strands across the middle. A few strands at a time, fold them in half and cut them in the middle, then lay a row of knots above the tabby (see *Rya Knots*) on each bottom weave.

4. Following the templates, weave in the background and then the image (see *Using Your Template*), taking it to the full 19cm (7½in) height before locking off with a hemstitch (see *Finishing Your Weaving*). Two down.

5. Measure 12cm (4¾in) up the loom from the locking stitch of the weavings below. Place a paper guide between the two levels if you need to, and weave the next two designs, checking and re-checking that they are the same height as their sisters. (1).

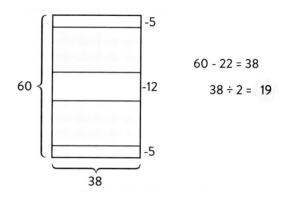

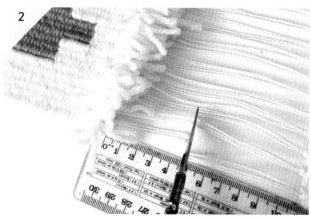

3

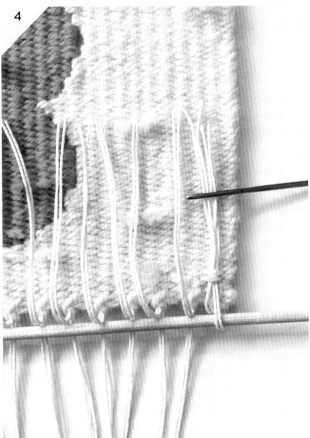

4

6. Turn your loom over to tidy the reverse, then start cutting the bottom warp threads (see *Finishing Your Weaving*) and lift off the top nails. Re-measure the space between the top and bottom weavings. You want to leave a minimum of 3cm (1⅛in) of warp strings below the top weaving to tie it off with, and at least 5cm (2in) above the bottom weave to loop around the hanging rod. If you have more than 8cm (3¼in), you're on easy street and can add a bit to those measurements.

7. Cut the bottom weaving from the top (2) and tie off the bottom strings as you move across. Repeat the process for the next pair of minis still on the loom.

8. Once all the weavings are off the loom and separated, pop some ladder stitch up the sides of any long vertical gaps (see *Embroidery: Ladder Stitch*), and add some embroidery embellishments if needed (3).

9. Measure the width of the weavings... they're all the same, riiight? Cut four lengths of dowel (see *Finishing Your Weaving: Hanging Your Weaving*). For those bottom weaves that have had their warp strings cut, never fear. Lay them face down and part the four warp strings in each knot into two pairs. Lay one down onto the back of the weaving, and smooth one up onto your work table. Lay your dowel along the top of the weaving, and thread the top and bottom pair of strings onto your tapestry needle then weave the four threads into the back of the weave as usual (4). Tie them off to the next group of threads along the weave, and continue with the technique as usual.

10. Tie your hanging string to each end of the rod, and give these babies a fringe trim. If the shorter fringe has kicked up at a weird angle, try using a hair straightener or iron (on the lowest setting) to help it sit down properly. Careful! Acrylic yarns can get a little melty in the heat – just like those ice pops...

Yarn Upgrade

If you're feeling like your yarn stash is a little lacklustre, never fear. There are ways and means to upgrade what you've got into something that little bit more special. Marble is all the rage, so we're gonna weave it.

YOU WILL NEED

> Your loom
> Tapestry needle
> Scissors
> Shed stick
> Beater
> Measuring tape
> A3 paper and pencil
> Drawing compass and ruler
> Spool of black cotton thread
> Round dowel for hanger

YARN REQUIRED

> Background and fringe: 12-ply light yarn, approx 60g (2¼oz)
> Split circles: Worsted yarn, approx 20g (¾oz)
> Half circle 1: Worsted yarn, approx 15g (½oz)
> Half circle 2: Worsted yarn, approx 15g (½oz)
> Cotton warp thread, approx 10g (¼oz)

COLOUR PALETTE

1. To draw up your template, lightly mark a vertical line down the middle of your piece of A3 paper, marking the midpoint of that line. Measure and mark 5cm (2in) out from that mark in each direction. These two outer marks will be your positions for your compass. Open your drawing compass so the point is on one mark and the drawing end is on the second (that should be a 10cm (4in) stretch). Draw one circle, then move to the second mark and draw the next. Remove the bottom quarter of one circle, and the top quarter of the other, and you have yourself two split, intersecting circles. Huzzah!

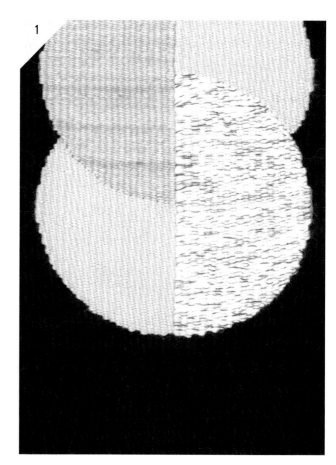

2. Centre your template onto your loom and double string the loom (see *Warping Your Loom: Double String Warping*), ensuring the circles are centred. I strung mine to a width of 29cm (11½in). Weave in your first 6–8 rows of tabby in your background colour (see *Starting Weave in Tabby*), laying your full density rya fringe above (see *Rya Knots*). Before starting on your background weaving, double check the position of your template to make sure the circle shapes are starting around 2cm (¾in) above the rya line, centred across the warp strings, and that you've got enough room at the top of the loom to finish the circles, weave another 2cm (¾in) of background yarn and do the hemstitch. Measure twice, cut once, baby.

3. Begin to weave up the loom, following the template carefully to ensure a smooth circle shape (see *Using Your Template*). Once you get to the widest point of the bottom circle (1), swap your yarn to fill in the bottom circle as follows. The left side will be the split circle colour, all the way up and around the curve of the bottom circle. For the right side of the bottom circle, grab the white yarn and spool of black cotton

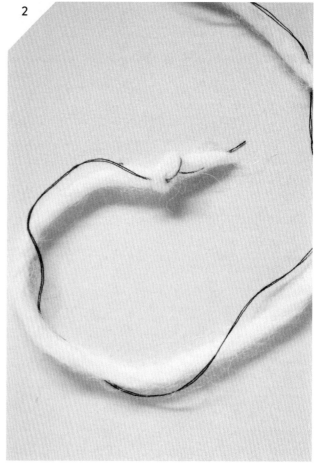

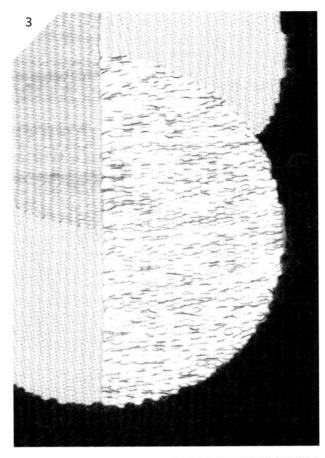

thread. Pull out about an arm's length of both the cotton and yarn, holding the ends together. Once you have a length you are comfortable working with, cut both the cotton and yarn then take a new length of cotton and tie a knot round the freshly cut ends. Run the yarn/cotton combo back through your fingers to unspool another strand of cotton to the same length so you have one length of yarn and two of cotton together (2). Thread the open end of the yarn/cotton combo onto your tapestry needle and begin to weave it into the right side of the circle. Treat the knotted end like a standard tabby tail to be woven in at the end. Make each new length of yarn/cotton combo that you need in the same way. In some areas the cotton will bunch together to be one thick black line, in some areas it will disappear completely behind the white yarn. Let it behave naturally and the random effect of marble will be magically created (3)!

4. Once your lower circle is complete, weave the background yarn up to the midpoint of the top circle, tabby weave in each side of the top circle and then weave the background yarn right to the top to make an equal amount of background at the top as there is at bottom of the design (4).

5. You know the drill, just follow the instruction in *Finishing Your Weaving* to even up, lock off, tidy and remove your weave from the loom (feel free to snip the knotted ends off the marble section to make them a little easier to weave in). As there is a large split through the centre of the circles, ladder stitch that gap up with some cotton (see *Embroidery: Ladder Stitch*) before you measure and cut your dowel (see *Finishing Your Weaving: Hanging Your Weaving*) and get it hung for your viewing pleasure.

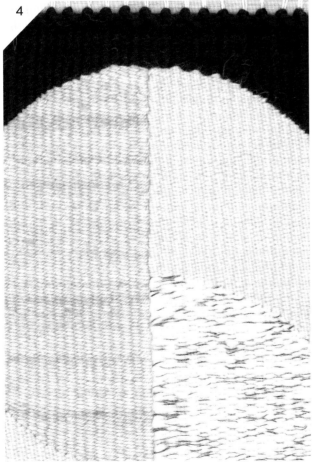

Your Name Here

This piece is a favourite of mine for gifts. If there is a new little babe born in your circle, this is a perfect piece for a nursery, or if a little one has a room re-do, here is a perfect little addition. You can customise it for the recipient through your choice of font, the colours of the accent yarn, even adding a particularly funky fringe, but whatever you choose, this piece will always be a winner.

YOU WILL NEED

- Your loom
- Tapestry needle
- Computer and printer
- Sticky tape
- Scissors
- Pencil
- Shed stick
- Beater
- Measuring tape
- Round dowel for hanger

YARN REQUIRED

- Background and fringe: Light/DK yarn, approx 100g (3½oz)
- Contrast colour fringe: Light/DK yarn, approx 40g (1½oz)
- Various accent yarns, approx 70g (2½oz) each
- Cotton warp thread, approx 10g (¼oz)

COLOUR PALETTE

1. There are two ways to create the template for this piece. You can freehand an initial on paper with your own creative superpowers, or you can use MS Excel or the like to create a template, by choosing your font, upping the size to suit your loom, and printing it poster style (see *Creating a Template*). Whichever method you choose, I suggest thickening some of the narrow parts so you have more room for the textured weaving. Just be careful to retain the overall shape of the letter (1).

2. Once your template is ready, set up your loom (see *Warping Your Loom: Double String Warping*), then lay six to eight rows of tabby using the contrast yarn (see *Starting a Weave with Tabby*) and a full row of rya knots in the same colour (see *Rya Knots*). Now using the background colour, lay 2–3cm (¾–1⅛in) of tabby before adding another full density fringe across the row, also in the background colour. This top fringe will be cut into scallops once the piece is off the loom.

3. With your double rya fringe in, just double check the measurements between the rya and the base of the initial to make sure there's enough room at the top of the loom to weave the same amount. When the weaving has one centralised feature, if it's off centre it's very noticeable. Centre your template now or forever be annoyed that it's a little off.

4. Start weaving up the loom, following the template up the sides of the letter (see *Using Your Template*). Once you've built up your background as far as you can, it's time to start on the textured elements. Here you can freestyle to your heart's content. Well, within the confines of that template at least. Curves look great with a soumak (see *Soumak*) fishtail plopped onto them (2). Large vertical areas can be broken up with some rya knots, bobbles (see *Bobbles*), inverted rya (see *Inverted and Continuous Rya: Inverted Rya*), and even some diamond twill (see *Diamond Twill*) if you've got the room. Use your textures and colour variations to create a patchwork of yarn. Step back occasionally to check if one colour has dominated, or if a part needs a bit more texture (3).

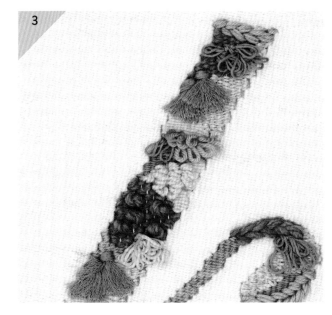

4

The smaller the scissors you use to trim the scalloped fringe, the easier it will be.

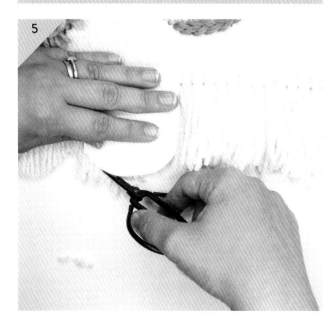

5

5. Work your way along the template, alternating between the textured area of the initial, and filling in the background. Once you get to the top of the letter, measure the amount of background between the rya knots and the base of the letter, and weave sufficient tabby to mirror that at the top so the monogram is centred in the background.

6. See *Finishing Your Weaving* to hemstitch the top, tidy everything up and remove the work from the loom.

7. Once you've mounted your weave on a piece of dowel (see *Finishing Your Weaving: Hanging Your Weaving*), hang it up and brush both layers of fringe gently into place. First give the bottom layer a trim into a nice straight line.

8. Now we're going to cut a scalloped pattern into the top layer of fringing. Measure the width of the top fringe when it is combed into place. Depending on the yarn you use, fringes tend to kick out a bit, so mine is 31cm (12¼in) at the rya knots but 33cm (13in) where it flares out. Work that maths brain and figure out how many scallops you can comfortably fit across your fringe. 33cm (13in) ÷ 5 scallops = 6.6cm (2½in) per scallop. Might be a bit tight. 33cm (13in) ÷ 4 = 8.25cm (3⅜in) each. Nice. Place a sheet of paper between the top and bottom fringes, so you don't get too scissor happy and start lopping off both at once. Brush the top fringe into shape again (4) and using the ruler to make sure it's even, trim the fringe into a straight line.

9. Now grab a scrap of paper and after measuring the top-to-bottom length of the top fringe, cut a template for your scallop the length of that fringe and width of one scallop (8.25cm (3⅜in) here). Give the top fringe another comb to make sure every strand is straight, then working from one end, lay the scallop template over the fringe and slowly cut to shape (5). Once the row is finished, hang it up and give any naughty little strays a trim.

Oh! The Texture!

Boom. Here is the ultimate in freestyle texture that will stop people in their tracks and make them want to run their hands through it constantly. Because I am a particular type of person, I like to have a rough plan before I start, but it's by no means necessary. Dive into your yarn stash and pull together a palette filled with a ton of different textures, shades and materials, and let your creativity go wild.

YOU WILL NEED

> Your loom
> Tapestry needle
> Scissors
> Shed stick
> Beater
> Measuring tape
> Round dowel for hanger

YARN REQUIRED

> Fringe 1: single-ply Merino art yarn, approx 50g (1¾oz)
> Fringe 2: chunky Merino, approx 50g (1¾oz)
> Roving: natural wool roving, approx 30g (1oz)
> Texture yarns: For example, white chunky Merino yarn, single-play chunky yarn, mohair yarn, 10-ply cotton, worsted yarn, approx 10g (¼oz) each
> Cotton warp thread, approx 10g (¼oz) in a contrasting colour to your chosen palette

COLOUR PALETTE

1. If you have the same mind-set as me and like a visual guide, draw up a simple little plan, picking the techniques you'd like to feature in your weaving (1). Sketch out where you're going to drop in some roving soumak, how large your diamond twill areas are going to be, where you're gonna chuck in some chunky rya knots etc. As there is no 'template' for this weave, you don't need the backing on your loom either. Simply warp your loom in a single layer (see *Warping Your Loom: Single String Warping*), making the weavable area as wide or narrow as you like.

2. Lay down a supporting tabby row first (see *Starting a Weave with Tabby*), and your first row (of what? One, two... three fringes?!) of rya knots (see *Rya Knots*). As you start building the texture up your weave, make sure to put tabby rows throughout, to support the loopy textures, to keep the weave flat and straight, and to direct or contain the different areas of floofiness that you're creating (2). Visit the techniques section at the beginning of this book for instructions on a range of methods for creating texture.

3. If you're going to aim for a swoopy wavy design, aim to highlight three or four main swoops or arcs across your loom, splicing in changes of texture and colour within each swoop, but capping off the majority of each section in the same technique and colour to draw the eye to the movement. Melding the changes in colour and technique into the swooping pattern will enhance the overall look, for example if you pop some diamond twill (see *Diamond Twill*) in the pattern try to avoid having a hard edge of ten rows of it all finishing on the same warp thread as it will stand out as a block of vertical squarishness in an otherwise curved and swoopy wonderland.

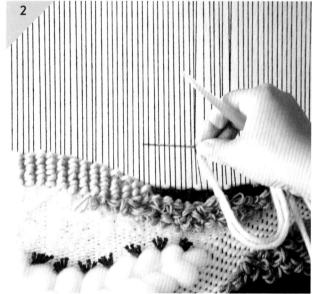

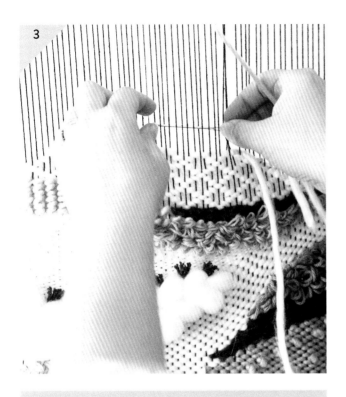

3

4. Build your way up the loom (3), flexing your creativity and trying new things. Make sure you allow for changes between your chunkier yarns (remember your weft-facing weaving (see *Weft-facing Weaving*) to give them room to move), the finer yarns (perfect for some rya knots for a scattering of tassels) and whatever else you're trying out.

5. Approaching the top of the weaving, I like to change to a simple tabby in a neutral colour so there isn't too much going on right near the hanger. Follow the instructions in *Finishing Your Weaving* to finish off, remove the piece from the loom and hang it. If you're lucky enough to be able to source something from the wild, these relaxed pieces look great hung on a length of driftwood or a branch from the woods. Make sure you go back and trim the fringe, any rya knots you placed throughout the weaving, and give any soumak areas a bit of a fluff and a lift before your creation finds its forever spot on a wall.

I like to use a contrast colour for the warp threads in a piece like this so the diamond twill stands out even more.

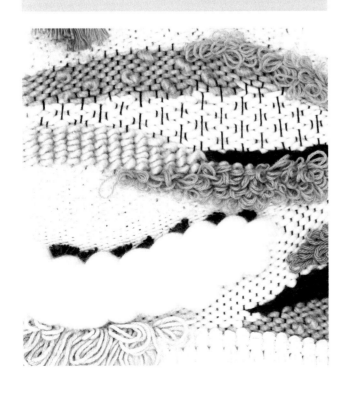

Milkshake

For our first foray into high-detail weaving, we're not going to worry about texture or anything too crazy. Just choose a favourite photo you'd like to immortalise – some type of action or quirky subject always works better than a straight vanilla pose. Think about what shapes are going on in the picture and how you can simplify the content but still convey the message.

YOU WILL NEED

> Your loom

> Tapestry needle

> Scissors

> Shed stick

> Beater

> Measuring tape

> Picture of your choice

> Computer and printer

> Sticky tape

> Felt-tip pen

> Black cotton or embroidery thread

> Round dowel for hanger

YARN REQUIRED

> Background and fringe: Light DK yarn, approx 30g (1oz)

> Background 2: Light DK yarn, approx 35g (1¼oz)

> Skin tone: Superfine baby yarn, approx 20g (¾oz)

> Shirt: approx. Light DK yarn, approx 15g (½oz)

> Hat: Light DK yarn, approx 10g (¼oz)

> Cotton warp thread, approx 10g (¼oz)

> Various other yarns for hair, lips, milkshake as required

COLOUR PALETTE

1. Let's start with some hot tips about picking your photograph. A simple background is best, so something not reliant on the setting. A woven portrait is quite quirky so an expression or an action that is also a little different is better. The closer the subject is to the camera, the more detail you'll be able to capture on the weave. You can add more detail to a weave of a head and shoulders than to a whole-body image. You don't want to make too much work for yourself so if clothing etc can be simplified down to a single colour, do it.

2. I used the hi-tech method of creating a template from a photograph (1 & 2), but you could also use the mid-tech version if that suits you (see *Creating a Template*).

3. Once you have your template constructed, and your yarn chosen, double string your loom to the correct width for your template (see *Warping Your Loom: Double String Warping*). As always, you need to start off with that base layer of tabby (see *Starting a Weave with Tabby*) and the rya knot fringe (see *Rya Knots*), before you start following the template up and up along all the detailed curves and colour changes needed by the template (see *Using Your Template*). As you fill in areas

that have details to be embroidered in later, i.e. nose and chin, weave over the area as normal so you have a solid base of colour to work with later. No need to leave gaps in the weave for the features (3).

4. Once you've made your way to the top of your template, measure the sides to check that things are level, hemstitch along the top and then do what you need to do to tidy the ends and get it off the loom (see *Finishing Your Weaving*).

5. First task once the piece is off the loom is to review the weaving for any areas that need the helping hand of a ladder stitch here and there, such as the sides of the hat to strengthen it and stop it gaping open (see *Embroidery: Ladder Stitch*) (4). Before embroidering the detail, take the steps required to hang the weaving on its dowel, so all the ends of threads are tidied and out of the way (see *Finishing Your Weaving: Hanging Your Weaving*). More than a few times I have embroidered a hanging warp thread into someone's face and cursed my brain.

6. The final step is the embroidery (see *Embroidery: Back Stitch*). Portrait weaves need to stay faithful to the plan, and accurate embroidery is paramount. For some of the more general areas of your weave such as adding line details into clothing for creases etc, you can freestyle to a degree, eyeballing where the line should start and end as indicated by the template. As you get to details on the face though it can be easy to stray from the template and then you end up with the face of a stranger. For those important and tricky facial features, cut apart your weaving template, around those difficult curves, and hold them against your weave as you backstitch along the lines they guide you (5). If it's a particularly large area or you don't have three arms, you can secure the template guide to the weave with a straight pin while you stitch the lines of the drawing in place. Take your time. The smaller the stitches, the finer the curves.

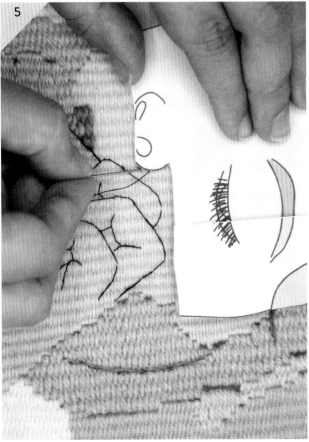

The Lovers

It's portrait time again, but on this occasion we're ramping up the oomph factor and adding some texture. Who doesn't want to be able to sink their fingers into the fluffy moustache of their beloved? Who needs to translate their curls to full-blown swirly perfection? Let's make those portraits jump off the wall with some real personality.

YOU WILL NEED

> Your loom
> A photo to work from
> Computer and printer
> Sticky tape
> Tapestry needle
> Scissors
> Shed stick
> Beater
> Measuring tape
> Round dowel for hanger

YARN REQUIRED

> Background: Light DK yarn, approx 30g (1oz)
> Fringe: Light DK yarn, approx 10g (¼oz)
> Skin tone: Superfine baby yarn, approx 20g (¾oz)
> Clothing: Light DK yarns, approx 15g (½oz) each
> Hair/Beard: Light DK yarns, approx 20g (¾oz) each
> Cotton warp thread, approx 10g (¼oz)

COLOUR PALETTE

1. First of all, we need to create a template from your picture. Open a copy of the pic on your computer and check out *Creating a Template*. For this piece, I used the hi-tech method. Remember that you don't need to include every single detail as that will make the weaving way more complicated than it needs to be. Focus on the main elements. The facial features, the hair shape, the overall shape of the clothing (1 & 2).

2. Secure your finished template to the back of your loom and double string the loom (see *Warping Your Loom: Double String Warping*). Make tabby rows (see *Starting a Weave with Tabby*), rya knots (see *Rya Knots*), and then get cracking on following that template up the loom (see *Using Your Template*). There are plenty of options for using texture on these portrait pieces. You can enhance the clothing with some bobbles (see *Bobbles*) or a diamond twill pattern (see *Diamond Twill*). You can use the inverted rya technique (see *Inverted and Continuous Rya: Inverted Rya*) to give a rug-like texture to a moustache (3). You can use continuous rya (see *Inverted and Continuous Rya: Continuous Rya*) for curly hair or overweaving (see *Overweaving*) to highlight the overall movement of hair. If you want to be particularly cruel to your subject, you can go in with some inverted ryas for the eyebrows and make them question how you truly feel about them...

3. Do make allowances for the thickness of the yarns you use for the textured areas. Every second warp string is enough for continuous rya. Check that you're not overloading the knot with inverted rya. Make sure you're weaving in some supporting tabby lines amongst each row of these textured rows to both support and space the effect (4).

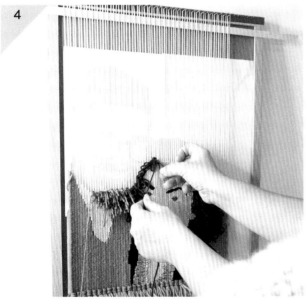

If you've got some cool threads like special metallic yarn or glitter thread, pair it with your yarn and give the clothing some extra sparkle.

4. Once the textures are in and the weaving is finished, run through the standard steps to tidy and get the piece off the loom (see *Finishing Your Weaving*). Run your eye over the piece to check if there are any areas that need some extra love and care with some ladder stitch here and there (see *Embroidery: Ladder Stitch*) and trim up any beard fuzz. Before starting the embroidery, finish mounting the weave on its dowel and tidy it up (see *Finishing Your Weaving*) before you go accidentally embroidering a warp thread into the piece permanently.

5. Last but not least comes the embroidery of the finer details (see *Embroidery: Back Stitch*). You can be a little liberal about where you put the larger lines like elbow creases, but for the finer details like jaw shape and nose placement I like to cut apart the template, cutting around the face shapes and embroidering against them onto the weave as a guide (see *Milkshake: step 6*). For the tricky curvy areas, you can secure the guide with a straight pin, or just lay the weaving on a flat surface and gently work your way across or up the weave, piecing in the details as the cherry on top of the weaving (5).

Fur Gets on Everything

Friends, meet Carter (no relation). All you animal lovers out there know that your pet is just another member of your family, so why not turn them into a piece of art as well? When you're picking the right image, look for one that gives you a bit of colour contrast, some movement and lots of personality. You might want to choose a standard worsted yarn and overweave it, but for this fluffy fella I'm using some lovely mohair yarn to give him the right type of 'floof'.

YOU WILL NEED

> Picture of your furry friend

> Computer and printer

> Pencil

> Felt-tip pen

> Your loom

> Tapestry needle

> Scissors

> Shed stick

> Beater

> Marker

> Measuring tape

> Round dowel for hanger

YARN REQUIRED

> Background and fringe: Chunky yarn, approx 80g (3oz)

> Base: Light/Medium yarn, approx 40g (1½oz)

> Fur details: Mohair/Bouclé yarn, approx 40g (1½oz)

> Cotton warp thread, approx 10g (¼oz)

> Embroidery cotton for facial/hair details: small amounts as required

COLOUR PALETTE

1. To create this template, I used Microsoft Excel to crop and resize an existing picture from my computer to the right size for my loom and printed it in greyscale. Then once the poster pieces were put together with tape, I went over the image with a felt-tip pen (see *Creating a Template: Mid-tech Photo Template*) (1 & 2). With the template in place, double string your loom to size (see *Warping Your Loom: Double String Warping*).

2. Using the background colour, lay the first 6–8 rows of tabby (see *Starting a Weave with Tabby*). I wanted the subject to be the hero for this piece, so I put half-sized rya knots along the bottom for the fringe. Do this by using a 10cm (4in) rya guide, and cutting those strings in half again before laying the full row onto the loom (see *Rya Loops*).

3. Start weaving up the loom following your template (see *Using Your Template*). As this design will be over-woven with fluffy bouclé and mohair, you just need to do a standard tabby weave over the shape of the subject to start with. Be sure that you're using white for the white areas, black for black and so on, but this is one time when you can relax on the look of the weave, and just focus on getting a good base down.

4. Keep working up the template, weaving in the details of any clothing, the facial features and the collar until you are past the subject shape, and back to full background weaving. Leave a good 6–7cm (2⅜–2¾in) gap between the subject and the top of the weave so the design isn't going to look too jammed in at the top. Check the piece is even, and weave in your hemstitch to lock it off (see *Finishing Your Weaving*).

5. Remove the backing from your loom and get to work weaving in all those ends (see *Finishing Your Weaving*).

6. Before you start overweaving in the fur, it's handy to lay down a rough guide of which direction you should be working in. Grab a marker, and with the template next to you, draw in any areas where the fur needs to change like Carter's spots on his chest, and any shapes the fur should curve around like the hair around Carter's snout (3).

7. Using the primary fur yarn, start overweaving the shape of those curves and patches onto the base (see *Overweaving*) (4). While overweaving, you want to have as little yarn criss-crossing the back of the weaving as possible, so try to weave the yarn in continuous lines up and back across the area, passing the needle through to the back of the weaving through only one or two warp threads or rows instead of jumping right across side to side so you have long trails of yarns on the reverse. Also pay attention to the tension of your overweaving. If you pull the yarn too tightly, it will pucker the weaving when it is taken off the loom.

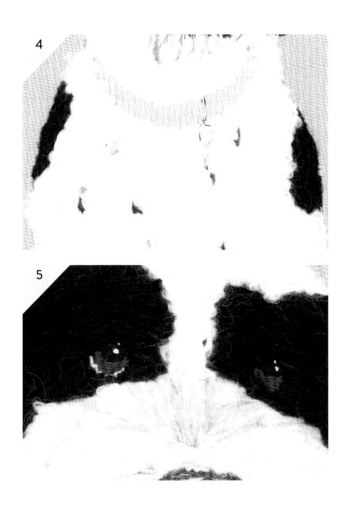

4

5

8. If your subject's fur has a large amount of colour change, build in the next colour along the shape lines of the first, and where your template indicates the darker or lighter colours of the coat will be. Be sure to trim the ends of the overweaving as you go.

9. Weave in those high contrast areas like Carter's spots by weaving in the darker colour over the patch you marked up earlier, then overweaving the original fur colour over the sides of the shape on your next pass to fill in any missing patches in the fur. As you use each colour for the fur and facial details, for example wet/darker hair around the mouth, you will be layering and re-layering colour over colour and in between threads to get that depth of colour and contrast. Once you're happy with how the fur is looking, the ends can be woven in and trimmed at the back. Remove the weaving from the loom (see *Finishing Your Weaving*).

10. Next embroider features such as eyes and perhaps a shiny highlight on a wet nose (see *Embroidery: Back Stitch*). Carter has some specific details in his original picture that I really wanted to enhance in his weaving, in particular his gorgeous, literally puppy dog eyes (5). Using some black embroidery thread, I embroidered in some dark pupils for his eyes so they had some direction in the glance, and then using a little bit of white, popped two little accent stitches in the eyes so they had some shine to them. I also layered some pinks onto his tongue, using the original source picture to guide me as to where the light and dark of the shape was naturally.

11. Finally, measure and cut your dowel and attach your weaving to the rod (see *Finishing Your Weaving: Hanging Your Weaving*). Trim up your rya fringe and there you have it – your own furry friend immortalised in yarn!

Remember - your photo is your guide. If there are some ridiculously intricate details on the collar that will drive you insane to recreate, just change it to a plain collar. Thousands of nuanced colours in the coat? Simplify it down to a few. The photo is a guide, and you are its master.

Templates

All templates need to be enlarged by 300%.

You can download full-size versions of these templates from: www.davidandcharles.com.

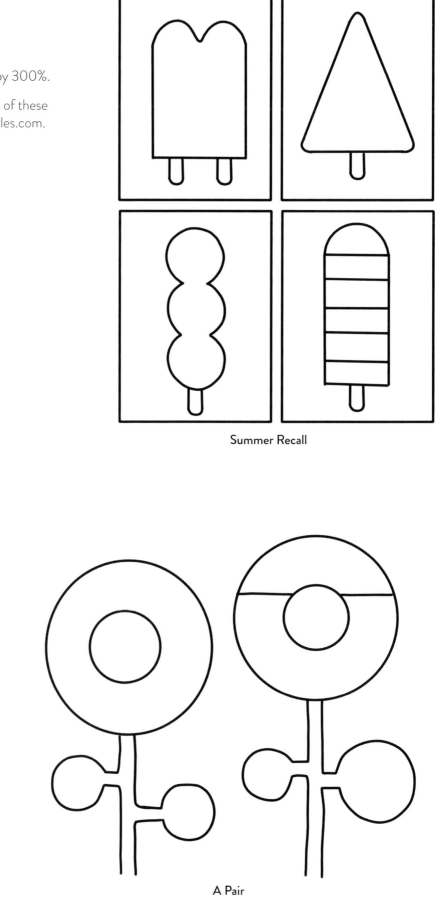

Summer Recall

Peace, Sister

A Pair

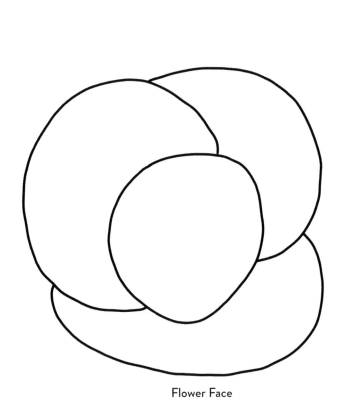

Flower Face

Girl's Got Hair

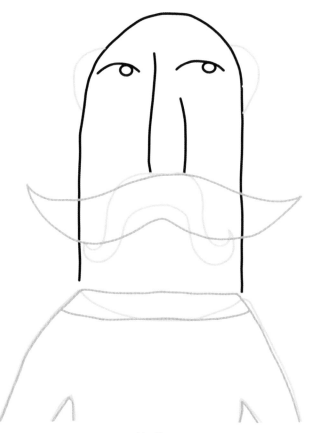

Mo Bro

Troubleshooting

Can I use a rigid heddle loom for this type of weaving?

Absolutely. Personally, the words 'rigid heddle' strike fear into my heart because I've never used one and it looks so complicated, but if you're that kind of clever, go for it. The main requirement for pulling off these types of designs is to be able to fix a template to the back of your warp threads and not have it shift around while you're working.

How should I sit when I weave? Does the loom lie on the table or do I prop it against something?

For smaller lap looms and the like, it is nice to sit in a comfy chair and work with the loom lying flat on your lap. The loom described in *Making Your Loom* is a little bit too big for that, so I would suggest leaning it against the edge of a table while you sit in a chair, or using an art easel or draughtsman board type set up to support your work.

Why does my weave bow in the middle like an hourglass?

That would probably be the tension, my dear. Be sure to not pull too tight when you're pulling your yarn through the warp threads. You want it to rest in its natural state as much

as possible. Bubbling your yarn in an arch above the weft before beating it down flat will help with this (see *Starting a Weave with Tabby*). As soon as you spy your work heading inwards, stop, unweave the section and start again. There's really no better fix for tension problems. Except perhaps a massage.

Why are there gaps between where the yarn changes in my weave?

Where you join colours vertically along the warp thread, you're going to get a few gaps. If they are noticeable, throw in some ladder stitches to tighten them up (see *Embroidery: Ladder Stitch*). You can reduce the gap by pulling tight on that first step above the joining warp strings, but beware of the rest of the row isn't tight or you'll run into tension problems.

Why are my warp threads visible?

Either you're not pushing down firmly enough when you're beating down the yarn (see *Starting a Weave with Tabby*), or the yarn is too thick to sit nicely against the other rows. Try some weft-facing weaving (see *Weft-facing Weaving*), alternating your overs and unders to give those chunky yarns some extra room to get comfortable.

My weave is wonky – one side is longer than the other.

This is an easy mistake to make until you get used to your loom. Be sure to measure the right, centre and left sides of your loom from the rya to the top row before you do your locking stitch along the top. If all measurements aren't equal, you will have to do some half rows to backfill the gap. Pop three to four rows of tabby on top of any half rows before you measure and lock off with hemstitch (see *Finishing Your Weaving*).

Why is the bottom of my weave curling up at the edges?

The number one culprit for this is the way it came off the loom and the bottom strings got tied. If you warp the loom up too tight on one side and then relax the tension by the time you've warped the other side, it can mess with the overall shape of the piece (see *Warping Your Loom*). It's the same when you tie off the warp threads at the bottom of the loom; if you tie one side tight under the rya and gradually get looser across the weaving, the edges will curl (see *Finishing Your Weaving*). Consistent tension always.

Should I use single or double warp?

It depends on what you want to achieve. Double warp is where it's at if you want gradual, soft, smooth curves, lines or other shapes. Single warp is all you need for more basic, blockier designs. Think of it this way – the more warp strings, the less pixelated your weave will be.

My yarn keeps snagging on those @#$%& nails and it's driving me crazy!

I'm with you. I've dropped my fair share of strong language over snagged yarn. My number one tip: once you've warped your loom with the cotton and before you start weaving, pop a line of masking tape or something similar along the nails and the back of the loom. This should save on the heartache.

I can't keep my tabby rows straight. They either dip off to the side or make a hump in the middle of the weave.

This is an easy mistake to make and easy to correct. All you need to do is tabby weave some make-up rows where the dip is, or on either side of the hump. As long as you've got enough tension in your work, the little corner turn of the make-up

rows won't be noticeable. But to be extra careful, if you're making up an error in a big area, stagger the make-up rows between a few rows of tabby, and across a few warp threads so it's not too obvious.

How do I keep my weaving clean?

I've had people ask if they can vacuum their weavings. Do they need dusting? No. The weaves should be so secure that if you notice some dust sitting on the dowel or the yarn after a few years, just take it outside and give it a shake or a pat.

What should I do with the leftover yarn after trimming?

There are so many things you can do with your trimmings. I organise my larger scraps into bags of similar colours, and when I have a whole bunch I send them down to a spinner who makes them into brand new scrap yarn and sends it back to me to go into another piece. Yay! You can also keep your scraps to stuff a pillow or toy. You can weave them into a patchwork or shaggy piece entirely made up of rya knots of scrap yarn. So many options.

What's the etiquette of copying someone else's work for my own home?

You've just purchased a book full of my work, with templates encouraging you to make them for yourself. Hurray! I love that you want to learn and have chosen my book to help you do that. I encourage you to copy the pieces from the book to practice your skills. That's what we're all here for. Things get murky when you introduce social media though. The assumption on social media is that what you post is original work. If you're copying a design for practice and want to share it with your crew, make sure you credit the original artist obviously and early in the post. Once you get your legs under you and want to start making your own designs, be sure to cast the net wide with inspiration to ensure that what you create doesn't lean too heavily on another artist's look. It's about being creative, not just copying.

Finishing Your Weaving

Alriiiiiiight. You've finished your design. You're happy with how it looks. Now you've gotta get that bad boy off the loom and onto a hanger, so let's go through the steps to get you there.

HEMSTITCH THAT TOP ROW

Ideally, you're ending the top of your weaving with 6–8 rows of classic tabby. To secure the top row, you want to keep a tail of at least four times the width of the loom in the same colour as your last rows, so you can lock it off with a hemstitch. This is a technique that can go in either direction, but for the sake of these instructions, let's work left to right on the loom.

1. On the front side of your loom, thread your tail of yarn (at least four times the width of the loom) onto your needle. Whether your work is single or double strung, we're working with pairs of warp threads – one up to the nail, and one down the other side. Starting from the left-hand side, bring your needle and thread around the back of the first pair of strings, out to the left (1).

2. Pull the thread through until a loop of a few centimetres (about four inches) is hanging at the front of your loom and push your needle through that loop from the top of the loop to the bottom (2), and pull it so it is secure.

3. Push your needle from the left side of the warp pair you've just tied, and bring the needle behind that pair and behind the next two warp threads, coming back out at the front of the weaving (3). Pull the yarn tail through completely.

4. Send the needle around this next pair of warp strings in a full clockwise circle (4) and down through the loop before the circle closes, pulling the yarn tight. Push the needle from the front left side of the new pair (5) to the back and curve it so it pokes back through at the top right of the next pair.

5. Continue this process until all the pairs have been secured together (6). As you finish the last pair, wrap the tail around into the back of the weaving and secure it into the tabby rows before snipping the end off.

Ensure you have enough yarn on your needle to weave a few solid tabby rows at the top and move straight into the hemstitch, which will need four lengths of yarn the width of your loom.

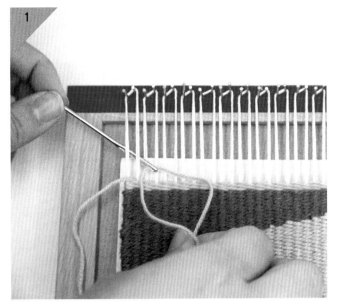

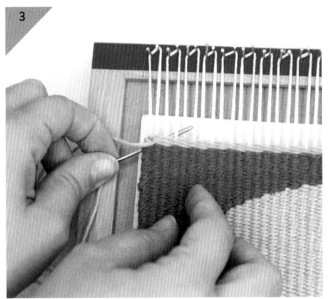

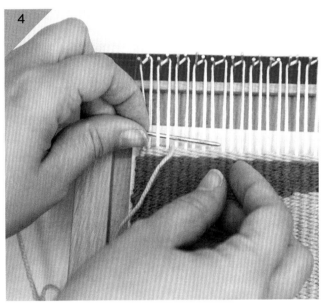

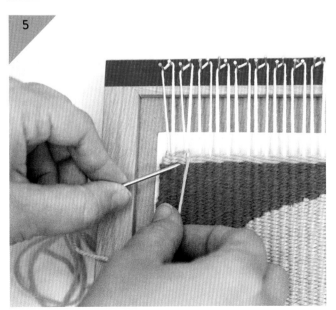

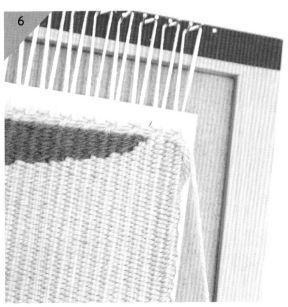

TIE IN THOSE ENDS

Now everything is locked at the top, here is your final reminder to tie in all those loose ends. This task is easiest when the piece is still on the loom, but can also be done later when the piece is off the loom and lying flat on a table.

1. First, remove the backing from the loom so you have easy access to the Dark Side of the Loom (1).

2. If you have any tails hanging out from the front of your piece, thread them onto your tapestry needle and push them through to the reverse side of the loom.

3. Where your loose ends match the colour of the weaving, thread the yarn tail onto your needle and push it under the next 'under' warp thread on the reverse side of the weaving (2). Pull the yarn through, giving each tail on either side of the gap a gentle tug to make sure there is no sagginess visible from the front of the weaving. If you're using slippery yarn or want to doubly secure them, you can then thread each tail onto your needle and push it through a gap in a row a few steps above, creating a V shape for extra strength (3).

4. If you have to weave a tail into a sharp turn of a shape, you can also weave it down through the row below, through the backs of two to three 'unders' (4 & 5).

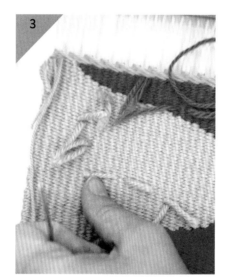

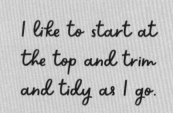

I like to start at the top and trim and tidy as I go.

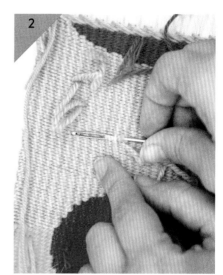

CUTTING IT OFF THE LOOM

Now is the time. The proof will be in the pudding to see if all that bubbling, tension attention and fandangling has paid off.

1. Remove the paper guide from the bottom of the loom and flip the rya fringe up (if there is one) so you have easy access to the warp strings at the bottom of the weave. Starting from one side and working your way across, cut four pairs of the bottom warp strings either between the nails or along the warp strings if you have the room (1). If the loom is double strung, each vertical thread should have two strings in it.

2. Starting from the edge, tie off the paired strings into couples using double knots (2). You don't want to pull these too tight, but have them all at a similar height and tension. Keep cutting and tying a few threads at a time so the weave doesn't lose all its tension in one go.

3. Once the strings have been cut and double knotted along the bottom, the top strings should just gently lift off the loom from the front. We're almost there!

4. With your weaving face down on a flat surface, thread each group of four warp threads that have been double knotted together, onto your tapestry needle. Slide the needle through the last 2–3 vertical rows of the tabby (3). Continue along the row, threading each group of threads up into the tabby row above.

5. Once finished, trim the warp threads to a 1cm (½in) tail (4).

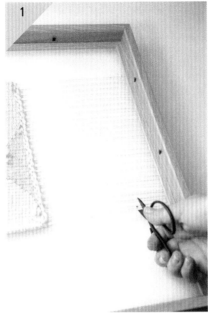
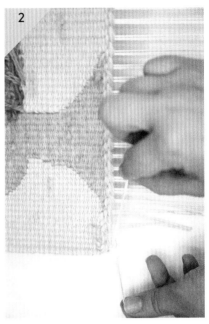
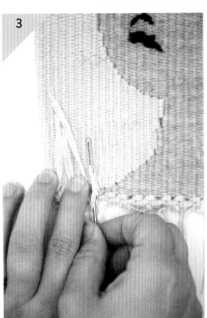
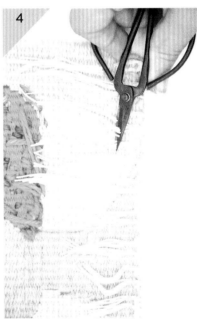

HANGING YOUR WEAVING

Hanging the weaving can be the trickiest part, and as with everything, there are a whole bunch of ways you can do it. I'll show you two ways here, and which one you choose will depend on a) how much fight is left in those fingers after weaving an entire tapestry and b) how short the strings are that are left at the top of the weaving. If you only have a few centimetres (or barely an inch) of warp strings left over at the top, you can simply use those as your loops to thread your hanging rod through and Bob's your uncle, it's hung.

Hanging rods can be anything from round pieces of dowel from the hardware store, a snazzy piece of brass pipe, pieces of driftwood scavenged off a beach, a funky coat hanger; the options are endless.

YOU WILL NEED

> 12.5mm (½in) circumference dowel

> Pencil

> Small handsaw

> Sandpaper

> Scissors

> Cotton warp thread, approx 60cm (23½in)

> Tapestry needle (for option 2)

Option 1: easy/short string

If you have enough length in your warp strings to loop them around the dowel twice, here is a simple way to hang your weave with a tidy look.

1. Measure the width of the top of your weaving. Add at least 5cm (2in) to that measurement to calculate how long your hanging rod should be. It can be longer, but 5cm (2in) gives you enough overhang to tie a string to for hanging.

2. Cut your piece of dowel to size with a small handsaw and sand the length and rounded ends of the dowel to make sure it is free of snags and splinters.

3. With the first warp string (the whole loop even if it's double warped), open the loop so it is flexed wide (1). Using your fingers, roll the loop down and back, so the top of the loop falls forward, and the two sides fold back on each other. The hole created from the middle part of the string and the sides gives you space to slide the rod through (2).

4. Work your way across the warp strings, folding and wiggling each loop onto the dowel (3). It helps if you use a rolling motion with the dowel to help it slide along.

5. Once the weaving is on the dowel and centred, cut a length of warp thread a little longer than the width of your dowel, double it, and tie it around the dowel at each end, using a double knot to secure it (4).

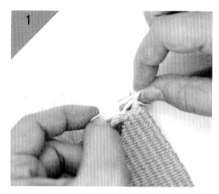

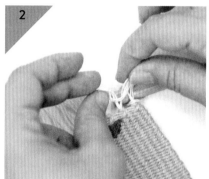

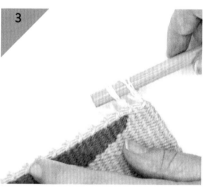

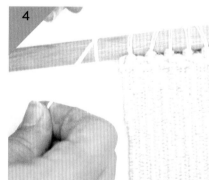

Option 2: moderate/longer strings

If you have more length in your warp strings, or you're using a hanger that isn't straight, try this method.

1. Measure, cut and prepare your dowel as in Option 1, and starting from one side of your weaving, thread the looped warp threads onto the dowel, twisting it as you do to help it gently on its way (1). Once all the warp threads are looped onto the rod, lay your weaving flat, reverse side up.

2. Starting from the right, thread one set of warp threads onto your tapestry needle (2), and thread them down into the back of at least two consecutive tabby rows at the top of the weaving (3).

3. Thread the next set of warp threads onto your needle and thread them into the back of the two rows of tabby underneath. Pull both sets of warp strings gently as shown so both sides of the loop are firm (4).

4. Tie the tails of the warp threads to each other using a double knot (5) – not too tightly, just so there's no slippage on the rod. Now thread the tails of the double knotted pairs into one or two rows below, and trim for tidiness (6).

6. Repeat this process with each pair of warp threads (7).

7. Cut a length of cotton a little longer than the width of your dowel, double it and tie it round the dowel at each end, using a double knot (8).

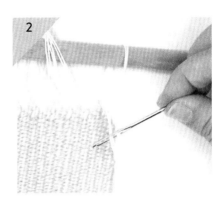
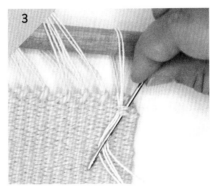
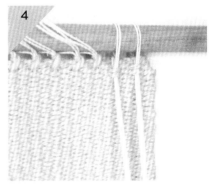
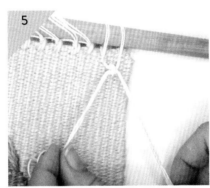
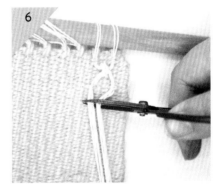

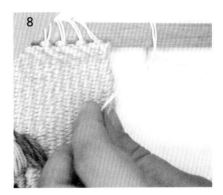

About the author

Kristin Carter is an Australian weaver, living in Northern NSW with her husband, two children and very old Schnauzer rescue. She is a self-taught weaver, yarn collector and indoor plant killer, who has been featured in publications such as *Mollie Makes* and *Koel Magazine*. Kristin began weaving simply to fill a spare spot on the wall in the lounge room, and kept it up when it became a creative outlet and something that was just for her, in the days of young family life when not much was. Kristin credits weaving with showing her that even the least patient person in the world can slow down and take things one unhurried step at a time. When she is not weaving, she is trying her best to avoid stepping on her sons' Lego, or diligently trying to open the chocolate wrapper quietly so her daughter doesn't hear.

Acknowledgments

I would like to acknowledge the Minjungbal people of the Bundjalung nation as the Traditional Custodians of the land where I live and create, and I pay respect to the Elders of the past and present. I'd like to thank the crew at David & Charles, as well as the wonderful Jane, for their advice, expertise and for guiding me through this process. The idea of writing a book was not anywhere near my goal list as a lowly self-taught weaver, but I'm so glad they found me and helped me through this journey. Thank you to Julie for all the pep talks and distractions during our long and backbreaking shoots, and unending gratitude to the cheer squad of friends and family that gathered around me to keep me going on the long slog, my always supportive parents, my sister Roxanne for knowing that doughnuts are always the way to celebrate, and special mention to my husband Justin who talked me off a ledge many times during this process, and was always there to run defence against meddlesome children who don't care that Mum was trying to write a book.

Suppliers

Warp thread from The Unusual Pear, www.theunusualpear.com

Yarns from various suppliers including:
What Mustard Made, www.traceymustard.com
Malabrigo yarn, www.malabrigoyarn.com
Spotlight Australia, www.spotlightstores.com
Texyarns, www.texyarns.com
Wool and the Gang, www.woolandthegang.com
Mary Maker Studio, www.marymakerstudio.com.au
Midnight Weave Co, www.midnightweaveco.com
The Australian Yarn Company, www.ausyarnco.com.au
and more.

Loom frames from BigW Australia, www.bigw.com.au

Tools from Loom & Spindle, www.loomandspindle.com.au

Index

A DAVID AND CHARLES BOOK
© David and Charles, Ltd 2022

David and Charles is an imprint of David and Charles, Ltd
Suite A, Tourism House, Pynes Hill, Exeter, EX2 5WS

Text and Designs © Kristin Carter 2022
Layout and Photography © David and Charles, Ltd 2022

First published in the UK and USA in 2022

ISBN-13: 9781446308943 paperback
ISBN-13: 9781446381182 EPUB
ISBN-13: 9781446381175 PDF

This book has been printed on paper from approved suppliers and made from pulp from sustainable sources.

Printed in the UK by Buxton Press for:
David and Charles, Ltd
Suite A, Tourism House, Pynes Hill, Exeter, EX2 5WS

10 9 8 7 6 5 4 3 2 1

Senior Commissioning Editor: Sarah Callard
Editor: Jessica Cropper
Project Editor: Jane Trollope
Head of Design: Sam Staddon
Designer: Blanche Williams
Pre-press Designer: Ali Stark
Illustrator: Ethan Danielson
Step Photography: Julie Willis
Styled Photography: Richard Jackson, Forever Creative Photography Ltd.
Other Photography: Paula Clark (114bl), Kristin Carter (106tl, 110tr)
Production Manager: Beverley Richardson

David and Charles publishes high-quality books on a wide range of subjects.
For more information visit www.davidandcharles.com.

Share your makes with us on social media using #dandcbooks and follow us on Facebook and Instagram by searching for @dandcbooks.

Layout of the digital edition of this book may vary depending on reader hardware and display settings.